THE HEART SUTRA

the heart sutra

THE WOMB OF BUDDHAS

Translation and Commentary by

RED PINE

SHOEMAKER & HOARD
WASHINGTON, D.C.

Library of Congress Cataloging-in-Publication Data

Tripitaka. Sūtrapitaka. Prajñāpāramitā. Hridaya. English.
 The heart sutra : the womb of Buddhas / translated from
the Sanskrit with a commentary by Red Pine.
    p. cm.
 ISBN 1-59376-074-4
 1. Tripitaka. Sūtrapitaka. Prajñāpāramitā. Hridaya—
Commentaries. I. Pine, Red. II. Title.
BQ1962.E5 P56 2004
294.3'85—dc22

                        2004011666

Text and jacket design by Gopa & Ted2, Inc.
Jacket art: Qui Ying, Chinese, Ming dynasty, 1494/5–1552.
*Chao Meng-fu Writing the Buddhist "Heart" (Hridaya) Sutra
in Exchange for Tea.* Handscroll, ink and color on paper.
© The Cleveland Museum of Art. John L. Severence Fund.
Map on page 19 designed by Molly O'Halloran.
Frontispiece: A bas relief carved from marble in 1956 to replace
an obliterated earlier eleventh century version at Lumbini,
where Shakyamuni was born.
Printed in the United States of America

 Shoemaker & Hoard
A Division of Avalon Publishing Group Inc.
Distributed by Publishers Group West

10 9 8 7 6 5 4 3 2 1

Contents

 The Heart Sutra

The Heart Sutra

1   The noble Avalokiteshvara Bodhisattva,
    while practicing the deep practice of Prajnaparamita,
    looked upon the Five Skandhas
    and seeing they were empty of self-existence,
5   said, "Here, Shariputra,
    form is emptiness, emptiness is form;
    emptiness is not separate from form,
        form is not separate from emptiness;
    whatever is form is emptiness,
        whatever is emptiness is form.
    The same holds for sensation and perception,
        memory and consciousness.
10 Here, Shariputra, all dharmas are defined by emptiness
    not birth or destruction, purity or defilement,
        completeness or deficiency.
    Therefore, Shariputra, in emptiness there is no form,
    no sensation, no perception, no memory and no
        consciousness;
    no eye, no ear, no nose, no tongue, no body and no mind;
15 no shape, no sound, no smell, no taste, no feeling
        and no thought;

no element of perception, from eye to conceptual
    consciousness;
no causal link, from ignorance to old age and death,
and no end of causal link, from ignorance to old age and death;
no suffering, no source, no relief, no path;
20   no knowledge, no attainment and no non-attainment.
Therefore, Shariputra, without attainment,
bodhisattavas take refuge in Prajnaparamita
and live without walls of the mind.
Without walls of the mind and thus without fears,
25   they see through delusions and finally nirvana.
All buddhas past, present and future
also take refuge in Prajnaparamita
and realize unexcelled, perfect enlightenment.
You should therefore know the great mantra of Prajnaparamita,
30   the mantra of great magic,
the unexcelled mantra,
the mantra equal to the unequalled,
which heals all suffering and is true, not false,
the mantra in Prajnaparamita spoken thus:
'Gate gate, paragate, parasangate, bodhi svaha.'"

Introduction

THE *Heart Sutra* is Buddhism in a nutshell. It covers more of the Buddha's teachings in a shorter span than any other scripture, and it does so without being superficial or commonplace. Although the author is unknown, he was clearly someone with a deep knowledge of the Dharma and an ability to summarize lifetimes of meditation in a few well-crafted lines. Having studied the *Heart Sutra* for the past year, I would describe it as a work of art as much as religion. And perhaps it is one more proof, if any were needed, that distinguishing these two callings is both artificial and unfortunate.

Whoever the author was, he begins by calling upon Avalokiteshvara, Buddhism's most revered bodhisattva, to introduce the teaching of Prajnaparamita, the Perfection of Wisdom, to the Buddha's wisest disciple, Shariputra. Avalokiteshvara then shines the light of this radical form of wisdom on the major approaches to reality used by the Sarvastivadins, the most prominent Buddhist sect in Northern India and Central Asia two thousand years ago, and outlines the alternative approach of the Prajnaparamita. Finally, Avalokiteshvara also provides a key by means of which we can call this teaching to mind and unlock its power on our behalf.

With this sequence in mind, I have divided the text into four parts and have also broken it into thirty-five lines to make it easier to study or chant. In the first part (lines 1–11), we are reminded of the time when the Buddha transmitted his entire understanding of the Abhidharma, or Matrix of Reality, during the seventh monsoon following his Enlightenment. We then consider Avalokiteshvara's reformulation of such instruction to correct Shariputra's misunderstanding of it. The basis for this reformulation is the teaching of *prajna* in place of *jnana*, or wisdom rather than knowledge. Thus, the conceptual truths on which early Buddhists relied for their practice are held up to the light and found to be empty of anything that would separate them from the indivisible fabric of what is truly real. In their place, Avalokiteshvara introduces us to emptiness, the common denominator of the mundane, the metaphysical, and the transcendent.

In the second part (lines 12–20), Avalokiteshvara lists the major conceptual categories of the Sarvastivadin Abhidharma and considers each in the light of Prajnaparamita. Following the same sequence of categories used by the Sarvastivadins themselves, he reviews such forms of analysis as the Bodies of Awareness, the Abodes of Sensation, the Elements of Perception, the Chain of Dependent Origination, the Four Truths, and the attainment or non-attainment of Nirvana, and sees them all dissolve in emptiness.

In the third part (lines 21–28), Avalokiteshvara turns from the Sarvastivadin interpretation of the Abhidharma to the emptiness of Prajnaparamita, which provides travelers with all they need to reach the goal of buddhahood. Here, Avalokiteshvara reviews the major signposts near the end of the path without introducing additional conceptual categories that might obstruct or deter those who would travel it.

In the fourth part (lines 29–35), Avalokiteshvara leaves us with a summary of the teaching of Prajnaparamita in the form of an incantation that reminds and empowers us to go beyond all conceptual categories. This teaching has with good reason been called "the mother of buddhas." Having survived a yearlong journey through the jungle of early Buddhism to the secret burial ground of the Abhidharma, I would add that the *Heart Sutra* is their womb. With this incantation ringing in our minds, we thus enter the goddess, Prajnaparamita, and await our rebirth as buddhas. This is the teaching of the *Heart Sutra*, as I have come to understand it over the past year.

KARMIC BACKGROUND

In the fall of 2002, I was working on a translation of the *Lankavatara Sutra* when my friend Silas Hoadley asked me if I would contribute a new English version of the *Heart Sutra* for a meditation retreat he was organizing just outside the small town where we live. I was glad to take a break from the *Lanka* and began comparing Sanskrit editions and Chinese translations and poring over commentaries. Although I had first encountered the *Heart Sutra* more than thirty years earlier and had read the standard explanations of its meaning, I had never thought of it as anything more than a superficial summary of the Buddhist concept of *shunyata*, or emptiness. I failed to see anything in it of interest beyond the line: "form is emptiness, emptiness is form," not that this made much sense to me.

This time I didn't even get past the name: the *Heart Sutra*. I discovered that there was no record of this title until Hsuan-tsang's Chinese translation of the text appeared in 649, four hundred years after the first translation into Chinese. This in turn led me to wonder how the Chinese word *hsin*, or "heart," ended up as the name of what has become the best known of all Buddhist scriptures. Since *hsin* is the standard Chinese translation of the Sanskrit word *hridaya*, I began poking around and found three Sanskrit works whose titles also contained the word *hridaya*. Known collectively as the *hridaya shastras* (a *shastra* being an exposition of doctrine by later followers of the Buddha), these were among the most influential accounts of the Abhidharma of the Sarvastivadin sect of early Buddhism. They included a work by Dharmashri (c. 100 B.C.), another by Upashanta (c. A.D. 280), and a third by Dharmatrata (c. A.D. 320). These three shastras were considered essential reading for members of the Sarvastivadin sect, and they eventually formed the basis of an Abhidharma school in China. I couldn't help wondering if their popularity had something to do with the name change that occurred sometime between the appearance of Chih-ch'ien's *Heart Sutra* translation around A.D. 250, when he gave the text the title of *Prajnaparamita Dharani*, and 649, when Hsuan-tsang titled it *Hsin-ching*, or *Heart Sutra*.

This inquiry into titles led me to other scriptures of the Sarvastivadins, and I discovered that this early Buddhist sect had compiled the Buddha's sermons into a series of texts known as

agamas, or "foundations." I found the *Samyukt Agama* of particular interest. Compiled around 200 B.C., this work contained all
the sermons of the Buddha and his most important disciples that
dealt with subjects considered worthy of meditation. What
intrigued me was that this work was organized according to a
sequence of subjects that corresponded exactly with the
sequence that occurs in Part Two of the *Heart Sutra.* Since this
sequence differs in the comparable texts of all other Buddhist
sects whose canons have survived or about which we know, I
couldn't help wonder if the *Heart Sutra* wasn't initially composed and didn't later receive its more popular title in reaction
to the Abhidharma of the Sarvastivadins. And this, in turn, led
me to embark on an inquiry into the Abhidharma, something I
had avoided ever since trying to make sense of Vasubandhu's
Abhidharmakosha thirty years earlier. As far as I could see at the
time, the Abhidharma didn't have anything to do with Zen, and
that's where I left the Abhidharma, at least until the fall of 2002.

This time I began at the beginning, with the word *abhidharma.*
Some commentators have interpreted this to mean "higher
dharmas," and others have insisted it means the "study of dharmas," or "dharmology." In either case, the higher dharmas that
are the subject of study are the entities of the mind through
which Buddhists gain their understanding of reality. According to such a conception, any given object or individual is
viewed as nothing but a construct of the mind fashioned out of
these *dharmas,* or building blocks of reality. In the past, some
Buddhists even held that such dharmas constituted reality itself,
which was true of the Sarvastivadins. But as I began exploring

the Abhidharma, I soon learned that during the forty-five years
of the Buddha's ministry, he taught the Abhidharma to only one
of his disciples.

This occurred just before the onset of the annual monsoon in
the seventh year after his Enlightenment, or in 432 B.C. (to use
the dating of the Buddha established by Hajime Nakamura). In
this year, while the Buddha was still in Rajgir, he told King Bimbasara that he would perform a miracle in Shravasti, the capital
of the adjacent kingdom of Kaushala, under the royal gardener's
mango tree. Hearing of this prediction, members of rival sects
preceded the Buddha to Shravasti and cut down all the mango
trees. But the royal gardener managed to find a single fruit and
offered it to the Buddha. After eating the mango, the Buddha
gave the seed to the gardener and asked him to plant it. Once it
was in the ground, the Buddha washed his hands above the spot.
As the water touched the ground, the seed sprouted into a huge
tree that burst into blooms that then turned into fruit. According to Pali accounts dating back to the third century B.C. (*Patisambhidamagga* I: 125), the Buddha sat down below the tree and
suddenly appeared at the center of a huge lotus flower from
which his image multiplied a millionfold. Then he rose into the
air with fire coming from the top half of his body and water from
the bottom half. This was then reversed, with water coming
from the top half and fire from the bottom half. This process was
repeated along his left side and his right side. Then the Buddha
stood up and walked along a jeweled terrace that appeared in the
sky. After sitting down and reclining, he finally stood back up,
and as buddhas before him had done following the performance

ance of such feats, in three great strides he ascended to Traya-trinsha Heaven at the summit of Mount Sumeru.

Trayatrinsha is Sanskrit (Pali: *Tavatimsa*) for "thirty-three." According to Buddhist cosmology this was the name of the celestial residence of thirty-three devas, including Indra, their king, and another deva whose name was Santushita. Prior to being reborn at the summit of Mount Sumeru, Santushita was Maya, Shakyamuni's mother, who died a week after giving birth. According to both Pali and Sanskrit accounts (*Atthasalini*, *Mahavastu* III: 115), out of compassion for his former mother, the Buddha spent the entire rainy season at the summit of Mount Sumeru teaching Santushita the conceptual system known as the Abhidharma, which is often described as "the way things appear to the mind of a buddha."

While he was on earth, the Buddha taught lessons suited to whatever audience he was addressing. But much like a doctor, his instructions were primarily intended to put an end to suffering. He never bothered trying to explain the system that formed the basis of his spiritual pharmacology, which was the Abhidharma. As later disciples and their disciples came to understand the Abhidharma, they claimed that it explained reality as a matrix (*matrika*) of dharmas, or fundamental entities of the mind, much like the table of atomic elements used in chemistry. From such a perspective, our familiar world of objects and persons was viewed as nothing but a conceptual construct fashioned out of dozens of these dharmas—seventy-five in the case of the Sarvastivadins. And to know things as they really are, a person needed to develop the ability to know the characteristics and connections among these entities. In his sermons, however, the Buddha nowhere advanced such a system, for it was simply too vast an enterprise to attempt on earth. Only on Mount Sumeru could the Buddha explain the immense and intricate scheme of the Abhidharma. This is because only such a place was sufficiently removed from the coarser levels of the Realm of Desire.

Thus, the Buddha taught the Abhidharma to Santushita at the summit of Mount Sumeru. But every day, he reappeared briefly on earth and gave his disciple, Shariputra, a summary, for a summary was all that was possible to teach or to understand on the earthly plane far below Trayatrinsha Heaven. Shariputra had distinguished himself for his wisdom, and the Buddha chose him, and him alone, to receive such instruction. Finally, after three months, the monsoon season came to an end, and the Buddha descended to earth at Sankasya, an event depicted with great imagination in Buddhist art, and he resumed his teaching but never spoke of the Abhidharma again.

Meanwhile, having heard the Buddha's complete exposition of the Abhidharma, Santushita advanced to the first stage of Buddhist attainment and became a *srota-apanna,* or one who "reaches the river," the river of impermanence. Among the Buddha's early followers, this was considered the first of three insights necessary for liberation. The other two concerned suffering and the absence of a self. While Santushita was cultivating this new awareness, far below at the earthly level of the Realm of Desire, Shariputra began compiling what he had learned into the first works on the Abhidharma. Early Buddhist schools attributed two such texts to this wisest of the Buddha's disciples: the *Sangiti-paryaya* and the *Dharma-skandha.*

The *Sangitiparyaya* is a commentary on the *Sangiti Sutra,* which is one of thirty sutras found in the *Dhirgha Agama* (cf. the Theravadin *Digha Nikaya*). This sutra was spoken in response to the disputes that arose upon the death of Mahavira, the founder of the Jain religion. To avoid similar doctrinal dissension, in this sutra Shariputra presents a list of basic concepts culled from the Buddha's sermons, and this list is approved by the Buddha as constituting the fundamentals of his teaching.

As to how this came about, Erich Frauwallner puts it this way:

> The Buddha had not preached a doctrinal system as such; he had demonstrated the path to enlightenment and had supplied the necessary theoretical justification for it. This represented the core of his message. Throughout the long years of his teaching, as he preached this message to an increasing body of followers, constantly adapting it to the capacities of his audience, certain concepts were also touched upon which formed a valuable complement to his basic message. However, since these concepts were dispersed throughout his sermons, they could thus be easily overlooked and gradually forgotten. Therefore, it is these concepts in particular which were collected in the *Sangiti Sutra* in order to ensure their preservation. These doctrinal concepts did not in themselves form a system. Nor was there either intention or desire to create a system from these doctrinal concepts; the aim was merely to record the

words of the Buddha. But it was only natural that a recitation of the doctrine, such as the kind contained in the *Sangiti Sutra*, could not simply be confined to an enumeration of the doctrinal concepts collected in the sutra. Some form of explanation was indispensable. The explanations of the *Sangiti Sutra* were eventually recorded in written form by the Sarvastivadins, and thus came to form the *Sangitiparyaya*. (Erich Frauwallner, *Studies in Abhidharma Literature*, pp. 14–15)

Although these explanations were attributed to Shariputra, they were continually revised and new interpretations added. Still, for such early Buddhist schools as the Sarvastivadins, Shariputra was the fount of all wisdom concerning the Abhidharma.

The *Dharmaskandha* was another seminal work attributed to Shariputra, and it was also composed around lists of basic concepts. However, here we are no longer dealing with a mere enumeration but with groups of concepts, concepts that were considered important for the practice of liberation or significant with regard to entanglement in the cycle of existence. Scholars have noted the similarity of the *Dharmaskandha* to the *Vibhanga*, a Pali Abhidharma text of equal importance to the early Sthaviravadins (ancestors of the Theravadins). Comparing the two, Frauwallner concludes, "We are thus dealing with a work from the period before the Pali (ed. Sthaviravada) and the Sarvastivada schools separated, a work which was then taken over and transmitted by both schools. Thus the *Dharmaskandha* proves to be a very early work from the time before King Ashoka's missions and can therefore also be regarded as the Sarvastivadin's earliest Abhidharma work after the *Sangitiparyaya*. But it takes the *Sangitiparyaya*'s superficial compilation of lists and constitutes the first individual work of the Sarvastivada school" (ibid., p. 20). Karl Potter reverses the temporal order of these two texts but agrees that both were compiled around 300 B.C. (*Encyclopedia of Indian Philosophies*, vol. 7, p. 179). Regardless of which text came first, both were among the earliest and most important works of the Sarvastivadins, and both were attributed to Shariputra.

This digression has been necessary not only to explain the focus of the *Heart Sutra* on the Abhidharma of the Sarvastivadins but also to explain the appearance of Shariputra in the text. Anyone who wanted to challenge the Sarvastivadin conception of the Dharma could do no better than to question Shariputra's understanding of the basic categories of the Abhidharma. And there could be no better person to do this than the Buddha's mother, or rather her incarnation as Santushita, for Santushita heard the entire Abhidharma, while Shariputra heard only summaries. With this in mind, I could not help but conclude that Avalokiteshvara must then be a subsequent incarnation of Santushita. As noted earlier, Avalokiteshvara follows the same sequence of Abhidharma categories used by the Sarvastivadins themselves to organize their *Samyukt Agama*, beginning with a consideration of the Five Skandhas, then continuing with the Twelve Abodes of Sensation and Eighteen Elements of Perception, the Twelve Links of Dependent Origination, the Four Truths, and finally the attainment and status of practitioners who follow the Buddhist path.

This conclusion, however, was just the beginning of my altered understanding of this heart of Prajnaparamita. The teaching of Prajnaparamita is also represented in the form of a goddess of the same name who has long been known as the "mother of buddhas." She is called the "mother of buddhas" because buddhas become buddhas as a result of their ability to penetrate and be transformed by this teaching, which is considered equivalent to the *dharma-kaya*, or body of reality. But if Prajnaparamita is the *dharma-kaya*, then Santushita must represent its realization, or *sanbhoga-kaya*, and Avalokiteshvara must be its manifestation, or *nirmana-kaya*, and the *Heart Sutra* must then be Prajnaparamita's womb, with our conception and subsequent birth made possible by the mantra at the end of the sutra.

A mantra is like a magic lamp, which itself is often cast in the shape of a womb. But instead of bringing forth a genie, as other mantras are intended to do, this mantra draws us inside, where we become the genie. Chanting this mantra thus creates the womb from which we are reborn as buddhas. This, then, is how my understanding of this sutra has changed over the past year. Altogether quite unexpected, but nevertheless inescapable.

HISTORICAL BACKGROUND

The *Heart Sutra* hardly fills a page, and yet it is the best known of the thousands of scriptures in the Buddhist Canon. Its fame, though, is relatively recent in terms of Buddhist history and didn't begin until a thousand years after the Buddha's Nirvana. During the chaos that occurred in China between the collapse of the Sui (581–618) and the rise of the T'ang dynasty (618–907), many people fled the country's twin capitals of Loyang and Ch'ang-an and sought refuge in the southwest province of Szechuan. Among the refugees was a Buddhist novice still in his teens. One day this novice befriended a man who was impoverished and ill, and the man, in turn, taught him the words of the *Heart Sutra*. Not long afterward, the novice was ordained a monk, and several years later, in 629, he embarked on one of the great journeys of Chinese history.

The young monk's name was Hsuan-tsang, and he set out on the Silk Road for India in search of answers to questions concerning the Buddha's teaching that this world is nothing but mind. In the course of his journey, Hsuan-tsang is said to have traveled 10,000 miles—west across the Taklamakan Desert to Samarkand, south over the Hindu Kush to the Buddhist center of Taxila, and down the Ganges into India and back again. And time and again, he turned to the *Heart Sutra* to ward off demons, dust storms, and bandits. When he finally returned to China in 645, he was welcomed back by the emperor, and stories about the power of the *Heart Sutra* began making the rounds.

This account about how Hsuan-tsang first encountered the sutra was recorded by Hui-li (b. 614) in his biography of Hsuan-tsang written in 688. Several decades later, the Tantric master Amoghavajra (705–774) embellished this earlier account in a preface to the *Heart Sutra* preserved on a manuscript found at Tunhuang in Northwest China; this manuscript (S2464) had been sealed in a cave shrine with thousands of other Buddhist, Taoist, and Zoroastrian scriptures in the eleventh century and was rediscovered 900 years later in the early twentieth century. Although Amoghavajra's version was clearly fanciful and historically inaccurate, it became the seed from which sprang the series of stories about Hsuan-tsang that eventually resulted in the Ming dynasty novel *Journey to the West* (cf. Victor Mair, "The Heart Sutra and The Journey to the West"). Hsuan-tsang also produced his own translation of the *Heart Sutra* in 649, and it wasn't long afterward that the first commentaries began appearing, as his fellow monks realized that not only was this a scripture of great power, but its summary of Buddhist teaching provided the perfect platform from which to offer their own interpretations of the Dharma.

Since then, the *Heart Sutra* has become the most popular of all Buddhist scriptures, and yet no one knows where it came from or who was responsible for its composition. Its earliest recorded appearance was in the form of a Chinese translation made by a Central Asian monk sometime between A.D. 200 and 250. The monk's name was Chih-ch'ien, and he was a disciple of Chih-liang, who was a disciple of Chih-lou-chia-ch'an (Lokakshema). The *Chih* at the beginning of these monks' names indicated that they were not Chinese, but Yueh-chih. During the second century B.C., one branch of this nomadic tribe migrated westward from their ancestral home along China's northwest border and settled in the upper reaches of the Oxus River (Amu Darya). In the following century, they spread south across the Hindu Kush, and by A.D. 150 they controlled a territory that included all of Tajikistan, Afghanistan, Pakistan, and most of Northern India, as well as parts of Uzbekistan and Kyrgyzstan. Since their territory straddled both sides of the Hindu Kush, it was known as the Kushan Empire, and it was one of the great empires of the ancient world.

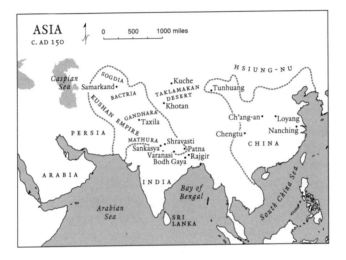

In their conquest of this region, the Yueh-chih made use of a network of roads first created by the Mauryan Empire (321–181 B.C.) of Candragupta and Ashoka and expanded by a series of short-lived dynasties ruled by Bactrian Greeks, Scythians, and Parthians. This network also served the purpose of administrative control and provided the revenue from merchants and guilds that financed the Kushan state. The same guilds and merchants also supported hundreds, if not thousands, of Buddhist monasteries along the same network of roads and towns, and Buddhism flourished under the Kushans. King Kanishka (fl. A.D.

100–125) even put the images of Shakyamuni and Maitreya Buddha on his coins.

Although Buddhist monks began arriving in China as early as the first century B.C., it wasn't until the height of the Kushan Empire, or around A.D. 150, that they began translating the texts they brought with them or that others brought to China on their behalf. The Yueh-chih monk Chih-lou-chia-ch'an is said to have begun working in the Han dynasty capital of Loyang around this time on some of the earliest known scriptures of Mahayana Buddhism, including the *Perfection of Wisdom in Eight Thousand Lines*. Between A.D. 200 and 250, his disciple's disciple, Chih-ch'ien, also translated a number of Mahayana scriptures, including the first translations of the *Vimalakirti Sutra* and the *Longer Sukhava-tivyuha Sutra* of Pure Land Buddhism, as well as a second rendition of the *Perfection of Wisdom in Eight Thousand Lines* and the first translation of the *Heart Sutra*, which he titled the *Prajnaparamita Dharani*.

In his *Maha Prajnaparamita Shastra*, written at the end of the second century A.D., Nagarjuna says the ideas and inspiration of such early Mahayana scriptures, if not the scriptures themselves, originated in Southern India and later spread west and then north. Most of Northern India was controlled by the Kushans during this period, and such teachings and scriptures would have moved easily along the trade routes under their control through what are now Pakistan and Afghanistan, then north through Uzbekistan, and finally east along the major arteries of the Silk Road to China.

Although the teachings that make up the Prajnaparamita are

thought to have originated in Southern India in the first or sec-
ong century B.C., the *Heart Sutra* was most likely composed during the first century A.D. further north, in the territories under
the control of the Kushans: if not in Bactria (Afghanistan) or
Gandhara (Pakistan) then perhaps in Sogdia (Uzbekistan) or
Mathura (India's Uttar Pradesh).

Not long after Ashoka inherited the Mauryan throne in 268
B.C., he sent Sarvastivadin missionaries to Gandhara. Ashoka had
been governor of Gandhara during the reign of his grandfather,
Candragupta, and his decision to send Sarvastivadin monks
there was a sign of favor. The cities in this part of India were at
the center of a network of transcontinental trade routes and
among the richest in the subcontinent. Thus, it is not surprising
that the Sarvastivadins soon became the dominant Buddhist
sect in this region. Over the course of the next several centuries,
preferential patronage by merchants and the ruling elite extended their dominance beyond Gandhara to Bactria, Sogdia,
and Mathura—basically the boundaries of the Kushan Empire.
And since the *Heart Sutra* was clearly organized as a response to
the teachings of the Sarvastivadins, it was probably a Sarvastivadin monk (or former Sarvastivadin monk) in this region who
composed the *Heart Sutra* upon realizing the limitations of the
Sarvastivadin Abhidharma. This was Edward Conze's conclusion concerning other Prajnaparamita texts (cf. *The Prajnaparamita Literature*, p. 94), and most likely it was also the case
with the *Heart Sutra*.

As noted above, the *Heart Sutra*'s earliest appearance was in
the form of a Chinese translation made by Chih-ch'ien sometime

between A.D. 200 and 250. This was followed by a second version by Kumarajiva around A.D. 400. In his translations, Kumarajiva often incorporated whole sections of Chih-ch'ien's earlier work, and he may have done so on this occasion as well. We'll probably never know. Chih-ch'ien's translation was listed as missing as early as A.D. 519. Hence, it must have been Kumarajiva's version that Hsuan-tsang first learned to chant as a young novice. Later, after returning from India, he produced his own translation of the *Heart Sutra*. But except for making a few character changes peculiar to him and deleting a few phrases negating the Sarvastivadin conception of time, Hsuan-tsang followed Kumarajiva's translation word for word, which is what we would expect of a text whose spiritual efficacy Hsuan-tsang had witnessed firsthand and whose wording he was, no doubt, reluctant to alter. More than a decade after publishing his own version of the *Heart Sutra*, Hsuan-tsang and his assistants also completed a translation of the encyclopedic collection of Perfection of Wisdom texts that make up the *Maha Prajnaparamita Sutra*, including the fourth and final Chinese version of the *Perfection of Wisdom in Twenty-five Thousand Lines*, which, for the sake of brevity, I will follow Conze in referring to as the *Large Sutra*.

What has come to interest some scholars of late is that the first half of Kumarajiva's and Hsuan-tsang's translations of the *Heart Sutra* also appears in an expanded guise in their translations of the *Large Sutra*. This would not be unusual, especially since the *Large Sutra* is a collection of many separate texts and the passage in question is quite short, amounting to only about eight lines in the Chinese Tripitaka (or lines 5–20 in my *Heart Sutra* translation).

But while Kumarajiva's and Hsuan-tsang's Chinese translations of certain lines in these two passages are identical, scholars have noticed that the surviving Sanskrit versions of the corresponding lines differ in these two sutras. Although the significance of such differences depends on one's point of view, it has been argued that because they are alike in Chinese but different in Sanskrit, the most likely scenario was that the first half of the Chinese *Heart Sutra* was extracted and condensed from the Chinese *Large Sutra*, additional material added to the beginning (where the Buddha is replaced by Avalokiteshvara) and a mantra (already in circulation) added to the end, and the resulting Chinese text then taken to India, where it was translated into Sanskrit, resulting in the differences we see today in the Sanskrit *Heart Sutra* and the Sanskrit *Large Sutra*. Eventually, so this theory goes, the Sanskrit translation made its way back to China, where it was translated by others into Chinese again. A full account of this rather convoluted argument appears in Jan Nattier's article "The *Heart Sutra*: A Chinese Apocryphal Text?" (in *The Journal of the International Association of Buddhist Studies*, 1992, pp. 153–223).

Despite the brilliance and depth of scholarship involved in Nattier's presentation of this thesis, we are shown no proof that the *Heart Sutra* was originally composed or compiled in Chinese, that any part of the first half was extracted from the *Large Sutra* or any other Chinese text, or that the mantra was added later. Instead, we are asked to believe that this is what must have happened because certain lines in the two Chinese texts agree and those in the two corresponding extant Sanskrit texts don't, and it should be the other way around, with the Sanskrit texts agreeing and the Chinese texts diverging in the usual course of translation.

My own solution to this apparent inconsistency is to assume that the lines in question in the Sanskrit texts of the *Heart Sutra* and the *Large Sutra* used by Kumarajiva and Hsuan-tsang were identical. Thus, there was no need, nor any basis, for divergence in the Chinese. In fact, there is no evidence, only speculation, that the two Sanskrit texts used by Kumarajiva and Hsuan-tsang differed at the time they made their translations of this passage in these two sutras. The differences we see today in the two Sanskrit texts, I would suggest, were the result of subsequent corruption or simply reflect the existence of variant editions.

Conze noted that the *Large Sutra* must have existed in a variety of versions (*The Prajnaparamita Literature*, p. 35), and this is also the conclusion of Shogo Watanabe (cf. "A Comparative Study of the *Pancavinshatisahasrika Prajnaparamita*" in the *Journal of the American Oriental Society*, 1994, pp. 386–396). This variation among Sanskrit editions is further reflected in the differences in the Chinese translations of the *Large Sutra* by Dharmaraksha in A.D. 286, Mokshala in A.D. 291, Kumarajiva in A.D. 404, and Hsuan-tsang in A.D. 663, where it is sometimes hard to believe these four monks were translating the same text. For example, Dharmaraksha's translation occupies 70 pages in the standard edition of the Tripitaka, Mokshala's 146 pages, Kumarajiva's 208 pages, and Hsuan-tsang's 426 pages. Thus, we have to ask why we should believe a scenario involving one version of the Sanskrit *Large Sutra*, when there must have been at least half a dozen versions of varying lengths and textual coherence in circulation.

It is far easier to believe that the Sanskrit copy of the *Large Sutra* unearthed in Gilgit on which Nattier bases her argument has undergone sufficient corruption to account for the divergence. For example, in one of the two sets of linguistic anomalies cited by Nattier in support of her thesis (where part of the *Heart Sutra* occurs in Chapter Three of the *Large Sutra*), the Gilgit text misunderstands the subject, referring the categories of line 11 to "emptiness" rather than "dharmas" in the light of emptiness. That this is a corruption is evident from its divergence from the teaching of the chapter in which this passage occurs. Leaving aside the issue of how one extracts a coherent text (namely, the *Heart Sutra*) from a corrupt text, we should not be surprised to find agreement between two Chinese texts and disagreement between the Sanskrit texts upon which they were supposedly based when one of the Sanskrit texts is either corrupt or represents a textual tradition different from the one on which the Chinese translation was actually based.

I have lingered at length over this matter because the contention that the *Heart Sutra* was originally compiled in China, albeit of Sanskrit pieces originally brought from India, has found a number of advocates among prominent buddhologists. Hopefully, as ancient manuscripts continue to be unearthed (alas, by explosives and those seeking sanctuary) in the region where this sutra was most likely composed, we may well see evidence someday that will clarify this issue of origin. Until then, we will have to make do with the knowledge that whoever composed this sutra bestowed on us all a great blessing.

In the years that followed the appearance of Hsuan-tsang's *Heart Sutra*, this text continued to attract the attention of translators. Fang K'uang-ch'ang lists twenty-one different versions in Chinese (cf. *Po-jo-hsin-ching yi-chu-chi-ch'eng*, pp. iii–xv). Although the translations of Chih-ch'ien (c. 250), Bodhiruchi (693), and Shikshananda (c. 700) have disappeared, those that have survived include one made around 735 by Fa-yueh. His was the first translation of a longer version of the sutra that included an introduction and a conclusion. This longer version, however, was clearly an attempt to give the text the stature of a standard sutra, and few Buddhists or buddhologists have accepted it as the sutra's original form. Hence, I have not used it as the basis of my own translation or commentary but have appended a translation of it to the end of this book for reference.

Not only has the *Heart Sutra* attracted the interest of translators, it has also been the subject of numerous commentaries. In Chinese alone, over one hundred are recorded prior to modern times, and of these more than eighty still exist. As the *Heart Sutra* was not well-known prior to Hsuan-tsang's translation of 649, no commentaries are recorded during the first four hundred years of its existence in China—though we do have a Chinese translation of one attributed to Deva, who lived in India in the third century. Also, no commentaries prior to the eighth century have survived in Sanskrit or Tibetan. (The fact that no early commentaries are known is cited by Nattier as further proof that the *Heart Sutra* is of late Chinese origin, despite the fact that few commentaries exist in Chinese, Sanskrit, or Tibetan for any sutra prior to this period.)

More recently, the *Heart Sutra* has seen renewed interest, and over the past several decades dozens of expositions have appeared in European as well as Asian languages. In compiling my own explanation of the text, I have consulted a number of these works and have translated selected remarks from about a dozen Chinese commentaries, mostly from the T'ang and Ming dynasties. For reference, after each line of text in the commentary I have included the romanized Sanskrit based on Edward Conze's 1967 edition of the sutra and also the Chinese translation of Hsuan-tsang.

In his *Heart Sutra* commentary, Ming-k'uang says, "The Buddhadharma is not far off. It's as close as your mind. Reality is not somewhere outside. How can you find it, if you turn away from yourself? Whether you're deluded or awake depends upon you. Make up your mind, and you will be there. Whether you're in the light or in the dark doesn't depend on others. Have faith and practice, and you will soon know the truth. If you don't take the medicine of the Great Physician, when will you see the light of the sun?"

Fa-tsang says, "The *Heart Sutra* is a great torch that lights the darkest road, a swift boat that ferries us across the sea of suffering."

Red Pine
New Year's Day, Year of the Monkey
Port Townsend, Washington

Thanks and an always ready pot of oolong tea to Silas Hoadley for encouraging me to work on this sutra; to Andrew Schelling for help with the Sanskrit; to Hank Glassman and his students at Haverford College, Robert Sharf and his students at UC Berkeley, and members of the Cambridge Zen Center, the Zen Center of New York City, the Village Zendo, the Atlanta Zen Center, and the Port Townsend sangha for sharing questions and insights regarding this teaching; to Tom Kirchner, Victor Mair, Jan Nattier, Neil Schmid, and William Waldron for sending me articles and information relating to the *Heart Sutra*; to Lin Kuang-ming for his line-by-line comparison of 184 editions and translations of the *Heart Sutra*; and to my wife for supplying me with the Chinese texts and tea. Thanks, too, to all those who have continued to support me and my family while I worked on this book, including the Department of Agriculture's Food Stamp program, the Port Townsend Food Bank, the Earned Income Tax Credit program administered by the Internal Revenue Service, and the Olympic Community Action's Energy Assistance program.

The Heart Sutra

Prajnaparamita Hridaya Sutran
般若波羅蜜多心經

PRAJNAPARAMITA 般若波羅蜜多

THE TEACHING of this sutra is known as *prajna-paramita*. The word *prajna* is Sanskrit for "wisdom" and is a combination of *pra*, meaning "before," and *jna*, meaning "to know." From the same combination, the Greeks got *pro-gnosis*. But while the Greeks referred to the knowledge of what lies before us, namely the future course of events, the Buddhists of ancient India referred to what comes before knowledge. Shunryu Suzuki called it "beginner's mind."

In the centuries after the Buddha's Nirvana, however, the focus of cultivation was on knowledge, *jnana*, rather than *prajna*. The members of the earliest Buddhist sects held that reality was a complex system of dharmas that could be known and that liberation depended on such knowledge. One of the earliest and most important texts of the Sarvastivadins was Katyayaniputra's *Abhidharma Jnana-prasthana* (The Source of Knowledge through the Study of Dharmas), which was compiled around 200 B.C. and which set forth a matrix of dharmas as the basis of all that we know or can know. It would appear that it was in reaction to this emphasis on *jnana* that the compilation of *prajna* texts occurred, focusing on wisdom as opposed to knowledge. Although opinions vary as to when the text before us was compiled, the use of *prajna* in the title tells us this is a text that goes beyond the analysis of reality into discrete, knowable entities, such as those used by the Sarvastivadins. Thus, Zen masters ask their students to show them their original face, their face before they were born.

Buddhists distinguish three levels of prajna, or wisdom. The first level is mundane wisdom, which views what is impermanent as permanent, what is impure as pure, and what has no self as having a self. This form of wisdom is common to the beings of every world, and despite its erroneous nature, it is by this means that most beings live out their lives.

The second level of prajna is metaphysical wisdom, which views what appears to be permanent as impermanent, what appears to be pure as impure, and what appears to have a self as having no self. This is the higher wisdom of those who cultivate meditation and philosophy and is characteristic of such early Buddhist sects as the Sarvastivadins. Despite providing its possessors with insight into a higher reality, such wisdom remains rooted in dialectics and does not result in enlightenment. At best it leads to an end of passion and no further rebirth.

The third level of prajna is transcendent wisdom, which views all things, whether mundane or metaphysical, as neither permanent nor impermanent, as neither pure nor impure, as neither having a self nor not having a self, as inconceivable and inexpressible. While mundane wisdom and metaphysical wisdom result in attachment to views, and thus knowledge, transcendent wisdom remains free of views because it is based on the insight that all things, both objects and dharmas, are empty of anything self-existent. Thus, nothing can be characterized as permanent, pure, or having a self. And yet, neither can anything be characterized as impermanent, impure, or lacking a self. This is because there is nothing to which we might point and say, "This is permanent or impermanent, this is pure or impure, this has a self or does not have a self." Such ineffable wisdom was not unknown among early Buddhists, but, if the written record is any indication, it did not attract much attention until such scriptures as the *Heart Sutra* began to appear four or five hundred years after the Buddha's Nirvana.

To distinguish this third level of *prajna* from mundane and metaphysical wisdom, it was called *prajna-paramita*. According to early commentators, there were two possible derivations, and thus meanings, for *paramita*. In Prajnaparamita scriptures like the *Diamond Sutra*, it is evident from usage elsewhere in the same text that the author derived *paramita* from *parama*, meaning "highest point," and that *paramita* means "perfection." Thus, *prajna-paramita* means "perfection of wisdom." But we can also deduce from the use of *para* in the mantra at the end of the *Heart Sutra* that the author of this text interpreted the word *paramita* as a combination of *para*, meaning "beyond," and *ita*, meaning "gone," and read the *m* after *para* as an accusative case ending. Thus, according to this interpretation, *paramita* means "what has gone beyond" or "what is transcendent" or, according to Chinese translators and commentators, "what leads us to the other shore." Also, because *ita* here is feminine, *paramita* means "she who has gone beyond" or "she who leads us to the other shore," the "she" in this case referring to Prajnaparamita, the personified Goddess of Wisdom. Commentators have long been divided over these two interpretations. Since both have their merits, I have used both. But I have also avoided both and have usually taken refuge in transliteration.

In addition to viewing prajna as having three levels, Buddhists distinguished three aspects: wisdom as language, wisdom as insight, and wisdom as true appearance. According to this conception, language provides the means by which insight arises. And insight perceives true appearance.

Chen-k'o says, "There are three kinds of prajna: prajna as true appearance, as insight, and as language. The prajna of true appearance is the mind possessed by all beings. The prajna of insight is the light of the mind. Once someone awakens, the light of the mind shines forth. And anything composed of words and phrases, regardless of its length, if it contains the wisdom of the ancients and dispels the darkness of ignorance, is called the prajna of language.

"Wisdom and delusion basically aren't different. This shore and the other shore essentially have the same source. But because someone thinks the body and the mind exist, we say they are deluded and they dwell on this shore. And because someone doesn't think the body and the mind exist, we say they are wise and they dwell on the other shore."

In discussing these three aspects in his *Diamond Sutra* commentary, Yin-shun says, "True appearances are not something that can be expressed by ordinary conceptions or everyday language. So how can we say they are empty or that they exist, much less argue about them? Nevertheless, true appearances do not exist apart from anything else. Hence, we shouldn't speak of them as separate from language. At the same time, if we don't rely on speech, we have no other means to lead beings from attachment toward understanding. Thus, as long as we aren't misled by provisional names when we speak of the nature of dharmas, there is no harm in using 'existence' or 'emptiness' to describe them. Some people say true appearances are objective truth, which isn't created by the Buddha or by anyone else but is realized by insight. Others say true appearances transcend such dialectics—that they are the absolute, subjective mind— the mind's self-nature. Actually, they are neither subjective nor objective, nor is there any 'realization' or 'true mind' we can even speak of!"

Te-ch'ing says, "What is the meaning of 'prajna' in the title of this sutra? This is Sanskrit for 'wisdom.' And what is the meaning of 'paramita'? This is also Sanskrit and means 'to reach the other shore.' The meaning is that the suffering of sansara is like a great ocean, and the desires and thoughts of beings are boundless. Ignorant and unaware, their waves of consciousness swell and give rise to doubt and karma and the cycle of birth and death, to bitterness that has no limit and from which they cannot escape. This is what is meant by 'this shore.' The Buddha used the light of great wisdom to shine through the dust of desire and to put an end to suffering once and for all. To cross the sea of sansara and to realize nirvana is what is meant by 'the other shore.'"

Pao-t'ung says, "The sutras say to cross a river we need a raft, but once we reach the other shore, we no longer need it. If a person resolves to find their true source and plumbs the depths of reason and nature, they will see their original face and instantly awaken to what is unborn. This is to reach the other shore. And once they are there, they are there forever. They don't need to return again. They will be free spirits unconcerned with material things, and they will be happy and at peace. Chia-shan said, 'The Tao is everywhere.' He also said, 'When you see form, you see the mind.' But people only see form. They don't see the mind. If you can look into the depths and think about what you are doing one action at a time, you will suddenly see. This is called seeing your nature. You can't know this nature through knowledge. You can't perceive it through perception. This nature has no form or appearance. When you don't see it, you see it. When you see it, you don't see it."

Fa-tsang says, "According to the *Maha Prajnaparamita Shastra*, 'Just as the great peak of Mount Sumeru does not quake for no or just any reason, the same holds for the appearance of the teaching of prajna.' Although many reasons might be given, I will briefly mention ten. First, it destroys the erroneous views of other sects; second, it leads followers of lesser paths toward the Mahayana; third, it keeps beginning bodhisattvas from becoming lost in emptiness; fourth, it helps them realize the middle way between relative and absolute truths and gives rise to balanced views; fifth, it reveals the glorious merit of the Buddha and engenders true faith; sixth, it inspires them to set their minds on enlightenment; seventh, it leads them to cultivate the profound and all-inclusive practices of a bodhisattva; eighth, it cuts through all serious obstructions; ninth, it results in the fruits of enlightenment and nirvana; and tenth, it continues to benefit beings in future ages. These are ten of the many reasons why this teaching has flourished. In the Dharma, we have the two categories of substance and function. *Prajna* is its substance and means 'wisdom.' It is insight into the mysterious and realization of the true source. *Paramita* is its function and means 'to reach the other shore.' By means of this marvelous wisdom one transcends birth and death and reaches the realm of true emptiness."

Several Chinese translations add the word *mo-ho*, for *maha*, or "great," to the beginning of this sutra's title. Although such usage appears in some citations of Chih-ch'ien's translation of circa A.D. 200–250 and in most citations of Kumarajiva's translation of circa A.D. 400, it does not appear in any other Chinese translation or Sanskrit copy that I am aware of. Hence, I have not included it. Another word I have omitted is *bhagavati*, which is generally understood as meaning "she who bestows prosperity" and, hence, "bountiful." Being in the feminine, it modifies *Prajnaparamita*, the personified Goddess of Wisdom. However, it does not appear in any Sanskrit copy or Chinese translation from Sanskrit and apparently exists only in the Tibetan.

HRIDAYA

In his *Sanskrit–English Dictionary*, Monier-Williams has this for *hridaya*, the "h" of which is nearly silent: "the heart or center or

core or essence or best or dearest or most secret part of anything." In titles, *hridaya* usually indicates that the work is a
summary. However, prior to Hsuan-tsang's translation of 649,
the *Heart Sutra* does not appear to have had the word *hridaya* in
its title; rather it was known as the *Prajnaparamita Dharani* (Chih-
ch'ien's translation) or the *Maha Prajnaparamita Mahavidya Dharani* (Kumarajiva's translation). Thus, sometime between the
fifth and seventh centuries, the text picked up the title by means
of which it has been known ever since.

My guess is that the use of *heart* in the title was in response to
the series of Sarvastivadin texts that began with Dharmashri's
groundbreaking *Abhidharma Hridaya Shastra* (Treatise on the
Heart of the Abhidharma), composed in Bactria (Afghanistan)
around 100 B.C. This was followed by a text of the same title
(and much the same material) written by Upashanta around A.D.
280 and another by Dharmatrata around A.D. 320 entitled
Samyukt Abhidharma Hridaya Shastra (Commentary on the Heart
of the Abhidharma Shastra). These last two texts were written in
Gandhara (Pakistan), and it might have been the second of the
two that inspired the change in the title, as it was the most influential Abhidharma text of its day in the same area where many
Mahayana texts are thought to have originated.

Another possible explanation for the presence of the word
hridaya in the title is that it was added to reflect the primary use
of this text as an incantation. While most commentators have
explained the appearance of *hridaya* as indicating that this text
is a summary of the teaching of Prajnaparamita, Fukui Fumimasa
has shown that the word *hsin*, which is the standard Chinese

translation of *hridaya*, appears in titles of other texts meant to be chanted and refers not to a summary but to the view that dharanis form the heart of Buddhist practice (cf. *Hannya shingyo no kenkyu*). A dharani, or mantra, is an incantation that possesses protective powers, and the *Heart Sutra* was clearly seen in this light from the very beginning, as the first two translations included the word *dharani* in their titles. Thus, during the T'ang dynasty (618–906), most Chinese referred to it as the *T'o-hsin-ching*, or *Dharani Heart Sutra*, and one of our earliest records of this text concerns its use by Hsuan-tsang to protect him during his travels.

Jnanamitra says, "Regarding *hridaya*, there is nothing profound or sublime in the *Perfection of Wisdom in One Hundred Thousand Lines* that is not contained in this small sutra" (Donald Lopez, *Elaborations on Emptiness*, p. 142).

Chen-k'o says, "This sutra is the principal thread that runs through the entire Buddhist Tripitaka. Although a person's body includes many organs and bones, the heart is the most important."

Te-ch'ing says, "What is meant by 'heart' is simply the heart of great wisdom that leads to the other shore and not the lump of flesh of mortal beings or their deluded mind. But because mortals are unaware they already have a heart that possesses the light of wisdom, they only see the shadows that result from their delusions. Instead, they take a lump made of flesh and blood as their real heart and cling to this body of flesh and blood as their possession and use it to perform all kinds of wicked deeds. They wander through life after life and thought after thought without a moment of self-reflection. The days and months go by, they live and die and die and live, and always subject to karma, always subject to suffering. How can they ever escape? Because the Buddha was able to realize his original true wisdom, he saw through the body and mind of the Five Skandhas as never really existing and essentially empty, and he instantly reached the other shore and crossed the sea of suffering. And because of his compassion for those who are lost, he returned to lead them through this dharma door of self-realization so that everyone might see that they already possess wisdom and that their delusions are basically void and that their body and mind are empty and that the world is but an illusion. Therefore he taught this sutra so that they might not do evil deeds but escape sansara and the sea of suffering and reach the bliss of nirvana."

Sutra 經

The Sanskrit word *sutra* is usually interpreted as deriving from the root *siv*, meaning "to sew," and as referring to a "thread" that holds things together, like the English word *suture*. However, some scholars have suggested that it might instead come from *sukta*, meaning "wise saying." Whatever its derivation, *sutra* was used by Brahmans and Jains as well as Buddhists to denote a scripture. According to the traditional account, Buddhist sutras date back to the First Council, which was held in Rajgir in the months immediately after the Buddha's Nirvana in 383 B.C. Many scholars now believe such an account was a later fabrication by early Buddhist sects anxious to authenticate their selections and interpretations of the Buddha's teachings. But whether or not such an event took place, these early sects applied the word *sutra* not only to discourses of the Buddha but also to discourses on the Abhidharma by later followers as well. As time went on, however, the word *shastra*, meaning "investigation," was used for Abhidharma texts, and the word *sutra* was reserved for sermons of the Buddha or disciples empowered by him to speak on his behalf.

In the case of the *Heart Sutra*, the text before us was not considered a *ching* or "sutra" until Hsuan-tsang's translation of 649. Prior to that, the text was considered a mantra or dharani, as reflected in the earlier translations of the title by Chih-ch'ien and Kumarajiva. Also, it is worth noting that none of our extant Sanskrit copies includes the word *sutra* in the title, and it is only reflected in the Chinese and Tibetan. However, since it has been customary for the past thousand years or so to refer to this as a "sutra," I have retained this word in the title.

Chen-k'o says, "A sutra points out what is constant and also points out a road. Demons and members of other sects cannot obstruct or destroy what is constant. Fools and sages all arrive by means of such a road."

Hui-ching says, "The purest emptiness has no image but is the source of all images. The subtlest reasoning has no words but is the origin of all words. Thus, images come from no image, and words come from no word. These words that are no words arise in response to beings, and these images that are no image appear according to the mind. By means of words that are no words, bodhisattvas spread their teaching. And by means of images that are no image, buddhas appear in the world. This sutra is thus the jewel of all teachings."

Part One
Prajnaparamita

1. The noble Avalokiteshvara Bodhisattva:
arya avalokiteshvaro bodhisattvo 觀自在菩薩

WITH THIS PHRASE the sutra begins, but nowhere are we told who heard or recorded these words. Most Buddhists attribute the memorization and recounting of the Buddha's teachings to his attendant, Ananda. But this is not one of the Buddha's sermons, and there is no mention of Ananda or any of the Buddha's disciples, other than Shariputra. The longer version of this sutra begins with the Buddha entering samadhi and with Shariputra asking Avalokiteshvara how to practice the Prajnaparamita. The shorter version, translated here, is Avalokiteshvara's answer. The longer version, however, did not appear until after the shorter version had become an established text. Hence, most scholars agree it was an attempt to establish the authority of the sutra by providing it with the standard introduction and conclusion in which the Buddha is present and the presence of his attendant with the unfailing memory is, thus, implied.

The question of authorship was an important one for early Buddhists concerned with authenticity. But over the centuries it has become less so. Nowadays Buddhists resolve this issue by considering the teaching contained in the text on its own merits. Accordingly, the principle of the Four Reliances (*catuh-pratisarana*) has developed to deal with this issue: We are urged to rely on the teaching and not the author, the meaning and not the letter, the truth and not the convention, the knowledge and not the information. Thus, if a teaching accords with the Dharma, then the teacher must have been a buddha or someone empowered by a buddha to speak on his or her behalf. For our part, all we can safely claim is that the author of this sutra was someone with an understanding of the major Buddhist traditions of two thousand years ago, the ability to summarize their salient points in the briefest fashion possible, and the knowledge of where buddhas come from.

The word *arya* (noble) originated with members of the nomadic tribe who referred to themselves as Aryas (Aryans) and who crossed the Hindu Kush and occupied the Indus Valley around 1500 B.C. A thousand years later, during the Buddha's day, the term *arya* was applied as an honorific to any person of high esteem, and among Buddhists it was used to salute bodhisattvas as well as the shravakas that Mahayana Buddhists would later denigrate as followers of the Hinayana, or Lesser Path. Thus, it was applied to heroes of early Buddhism regardless of their sectarian affiliation.

The term *bodhisattva* is usually explained as "a being (*sattva*) of enlightenment (*bodhi*)." But *sattva* also means something akin to "warrior," and a number of scholars have suggested the original meaning of *bodhisattva* was tantamount to "champion of enlightenment." In either case, the main advantage in using the term *bodhisattva* was that it represented a change in the focus of practice from nirvana, which was the goal of shravakas, to enlightenment. Thus, it eventually became the standard form of reference for the paragons of Mahayana practice, as opposed to the shravakas of the Hinayana.

Shravaka means "one who hears" and originally referred to those disciples who actually heard the Buddha speak. Later, it was extended to include the members of such early sects as the Sarvastivadins. And later still, it was used pejoratively by Mahayana Buddhists in reference to those who sought nirvana for themselves without concern for the liberation of others. It should be noted, though, that this depiction of the Hinayana was a Mahayana invention and doubtlessly included a certain amount of distortion of the actual practice of those at whom it was aimed, namely monks and nuns who followed the letter and not the spirit of the Dharma. Thus, a shravaka was often described as one who merely *heard* the teachings of the Buddha but did not put them into practice.

In the longer version of this sutra, the term *mahasattva* appears in apposition to *bodhisattva*, as it often does in Mahayana sutras. Literally, this means "great being" or "great hero," depending on how one understands *sattva*. Its earliest reference, however, was not to humans but to lions. Only later was it applied to those who shared the courage of the king of beasts. Although the term *bodhisattva* was used by other religious sects before the advent of Buddhism, the compound *bodhisattva-mahasattva* was used exclusively by Buddhists. It appears in such early Mahayana texts as the *Ratnaguna-sancaya Gatha*, a Prajnaparamita text usually given a date of circa 100 B.C. But I have also found it in the *Samyukt Agama* (1177), a sutra compilation of the Sarvastivadins dating back to 200 B.C., if not earlier.

The noble bodhisattva who delivers this teaching is not just any bodhisattva but the most revered bodhisattva in the entire Buddhist pantheon and the only bodhisattva with both male and female identities. The name *Avalokiteshvara* is compounded of four parts: the verbal prefix *ava*, which means "down"; the verb *lok*, which means "to look"; the suffix *ita*, which changes the verb *avalok* (to look down) into a noun (one who looks down); and finally *ishvara*, which means "lord" or "master." In accordance with the rules of sound combination, *ishvara* becomes *eshvara*, and the four parts together mean "Master of Looking Down" or "Lord Who Looks Down." Also, the short *a* at the end of *ishvara* indicates that the name is masculine. If it were feminine, *ishvara* would become *ishvari*. In Chinese texts, Avalokiteshvara is usually translated *Kuan-tzu-tsai* (Master of Looking Down), which was the rendering preferred by Hsuan-tsang.

In some Sanskrit texts this bodhisattva's name was also written Avalokitasvara. In such cases, it was translated into Chinese as *Kuan-yin*, meaning "He/She Who Looks Down Upon Sound (Cries)," or as *Kuan-shih-yin*, meaning "He/She Who Looks Down Upon the Sounds (Cries) of the World," which was the rendering preferred by Kumarajiva. According to this variation, *ava-lok-ita* is read as above, but *ishvara* is changed into *a-svara*, meaning "low, indistinct voice," or read as equivalent to *ahr-svara*, meaning "the sound of lamentation." While such etymological gymnastics are always possible in the old Vedic science of *nirukta*, or word interpretation, the reading required to translate Avalokitasvara into *Kuan-shih-yin* does more than bend the rules. Relying on the notion that there is an etymological connection between *lok*, meaning "to look," and *loka*, meaning "world"—the idea being that for most people the world is the visible realm—some early translator apparently wondered why we can't have both meanings at the same time in the same word. Thus, while *Kuan-yin* is the expected translation of Avalokitasvara, *Kuan-shih-yin*, presto-chango, is two words in one, which is not out of keeping with the powers of this bodhisattva.

Despite Avalokiteshvara's stature in the Buddhist pantheon, we know nothing about his origins. The earliest surviving statues (all of which depict a male form) date back to the third and fourth centuries A.D., and his earliest recorded appearances are in Pure Land sutras, such as the *Longer Sukhavativyuha*, translated into Chinese in the latter part of the second century. Near the end of the *Lotus Sutra*, which was first translated into Chinese at the end of the third century, the Buddha says that simply hearing this bodhisattva's name will free devotees from suffering and that chanting the name or thinking about this bodhisattva will save them from affliction, no matter how dire. For the sound of this bodhisattva's name has the power to echo through the universe and to make visible all who hear it, recite it, or recollect it. And as Avalokitasvara becomes aware of them, they are graced by this bodhisattva's infinite compassion.

Given Avalokiteshvara's appearance in scriptures as early as the second century, we can be reasonably safe in assuming that he joined the spiritual pantheon of Mahayana Buddhism no later than the first century A.D. and probably earlier. His origin, however, remains a matter of speculation. His earliest mentioned residence was on the mythical island of Potalaka somewhere off the southern coast of India, which is where he was living when he was visited by Sudhana in the Gandavyuha chapter of the *Avatamsaka Sutra*.

But if Avalokiteshvara came from Southern India, he gained his greatest following in the Northwest, where Mahayana Buddhism is said to have taken root in the century before and after the beginning of the Christian Era. This may have also been the area where this bodhisattva acquired several of his most prominent characteristics, and perhaps his female persona. One such source might have been the Persian goddess Anahita (the Blameless or Untainted One), who is often depicted, like Avalokiteshvara, holding a vase that bestows the water of life. Anahita is also accompanied by a peacock with a tail of a thousand eyes, not unlike Avalokiteshvara's manifestation with a thousand arms and an eye in each hand. The earliest mention of this bodhisattva's female persona, however, does not occur until the fifth century in China. Still, the fact that a woman could be recognized as an incarnation of Avalokiteshvara at this date suggests that the association goes back much earlier, though perhaps not in written form. Thus, we will have to wait for archaeological evidence to emerge from Central and South Asia before we can say anything more on this.

In addition to our ignorance concerning the origins of this bodhisattva, another question that has puzzled scholars is that

Avalokiteshvara is invariably associated with Pure Land texts or with such millenarian scriptures as the *Lotus Sutra*. And this bodhisattva's chief attribute is compassion, not wisdom. So what is he doing delivering this heart of the Prajnaparamita, or Perfection of Wisdom? Some commentators have tried to explain this by suggesting that since wisdom is based on compassion, it is only fitting for Avalokiteshvara to serve as the medium through which we receive this summary. I find such an explanation unconvincing. He is nearly invisible in other Perfection of Wisdom texts, appearing only briefly in the *Perfection of Wisdom in Twenty-five Thousand Lines* and in the *Purna-prabhasa Samadhi-mati Sutra*, and then in the background. And nowhere else does Avalokiteshvara teach this teaching.

Because no one has offered anything approaching an answer to this anomaly, and because of the reasoning I have outlined in the introduction, I cannot help but conclude that Avalokiteshvara appears here as an incarnation of Maya, the Buddha's mother. Thus, Avalokiteshvara's name, meaning Lord of Those Who Look Down from On High, refers to her rebirth as the deva Santushita on the summit of Mount Sumeru, where she gained the perspective and the knowledge that enabled her to look down upon such conceptual systems as the Abhidharma. That she now appears as a male bodhisattva is in keeping with the early Buddhist notion that such rebirth was necessary for the cultivation and attainment of buddhahood. However, Avalokiteshvara alone among bodhisattvas was also known for the ability to appear as a female, which was, no doubt, related to his previous incarnation as Maya. Another point worth noting is

that Avalokiteshvara is known to have thirty-three manifestations, the same number as the number of devas at the summit of
Mount Sumeru.

Fa-tsang says, "This name is given to someone who has the
power to see without being obstructed by concepts or objects
and whose power to see how to aid those who hope to be rescued is also unobstructed. The first explains his wisdom, the second his compassion."

Chih-shen says, "Avalokiteshvara sees existence but does not
cling to existence and sees emptiness but is not attached to
emptiness. Bodhisattvas can suck up the ocean in a strand of hair
or put Mount Sumeru in a mustard seed. A mustard seed and a
strand of hair represent the mind, while Mount Sumeru and the
ocean represent the world. Whenever a bodhisattva thinks about
Mount Sumeru or the ocean, they are in the bodhisattva's mind.
Thus a mustard seed contains Mount Sumeru and a strand of
hair the ocean. The reason this is so is because all dharmas come
from the mind."

Chen-k'o says, "Beings have never ceased to be bodhisattvas.
But because they don't understand that individuals and dharmas
are empty, and they become trapped by suffering, we call them
beings. Once a person's understanding is unobstructed, who
isn't a bodhisattva? Kuan-tzu-tsai (Avalokiteshvara) is another
name for Kuan-shih-yin (Avalokitasvara). Someone like Chef
Ting (*Chuangtzu:* 2), who could butcher an ox with his knife as
if nothing was there, is called an *ishvara*."

Ching-chueh says, "As for *ishvara*, ordinary people are tied by
dharmas to the pillars of the Five Skandhas and have no mastery

over them. A bodhisattva sees within that the Four Elements and Five Skandhas are completely empty and becomes their master. Seng-chao says, 'The attributes of dharmas neither exist nor do not exist, thus there is nothing to point to outside. And the knowledge of sages neither exists nor does not exist, thus there is nothing to think about inside.' If one can be like this, one dwells in existence without existing, because one doesn't think about the existence of existence. And one dwells in emptiness without being empty, because one doesn't cling to the emptiness of emptiness. When the mind is pure and unmoving, and the world is pure and unchanging, when one communicates without words and is obstructed by nothing, one is called an *ishvara* bodhisattva."

Hui-ching says, "Seeing the emptiness of greed, he is master of generosity; seeing the emptiness of sin, he is master of morality; the same holds for the rest of the paramitas; and seeing the emptiness of ignorance, he is master of wisdom. Seeing the Hinayana Path as a provisional teaching, he is master of the Four Truths; seeing the Middle Path as a sequential teaching, he is master of the Chain of Dependent Origination; and seeing the Mahayana Path as free of attachments, he is master of enlightenment and nirvana. Seeing form as empty, he is master of the eyes; seeing sound as empty, he is master of the ears; the same holds for the rest of the senses; and seeing the emptiness of dharmas, he is the master of the mind. Seeing the subject as empty, he is master of the interior; seeing the object as unreal, he is master of the exterior. Because he sees there is not a single dharma to be found, he is thus called a master. But any bodhisattva who is no longer bound by the twin dharmas of passion and nirvana is a master, not only Avalokiteshvara."

Yin-shun says, "This bodhisattva who has attained mastery over the insights of prajna does not necessarily refer to the bodhisattva of Potalaka Island (home of Avalokiteshvara). Whoever possesses the power of unobstructed reflection is worthy of being called Avalokiteshvara."

2. WHILE PRACTICING THE DEEP PRACTICE OF PRAJNAPARAMITA: *gambhiran prajna-paramita caryan caramano* 行深般若波羅蜜多時

The word *cara* here serves as both a verb and a direct object and means to practice the practice, to walk the walk. In early texts, the Buddha's disciples were distinguished as to whether they were still in training (*shaiksha*) or no longer in need of training (*ashaksha*), and the Buddha's teachings were referred to as a system of training (*shiksha*). Thus, Buddhism is better understood as a skill or an art to be practiced and perfected rather than as information or knowledge to be learned and amassed.

This practice is described here as *gambhira*, or "deep." The same adjective is also used in Sanskrit to describe the two bodily clefts of the navel and the vagina that link one life to another, and its use here recalls the Buddha's teaching to Subhuti in the *Diamond Sutra:* "From this is born the unexcelled, perfect enlightenment of tathagatas, arhans, and fully enlightened ones. From this are born buddhas and bhagavans" (8). Nothing could be deeper than the womb of Prajnaparamita, the Goddess of

Transcendent Wisdom, with whom all buddhas are linked, belly to belly.

In the longer, later version of this sutra, this is also the name of the samadhi (union of subject and object in meditation) in which the Buddha remains while Avalokiteshvara speaks this sutra: *Gambhira Avabhasan* (Manifestation of the Deep). As noted, *gambhira* refers to such bodily clefts as the vagina and the navel, while *avabhasan* can mean "illumination" or "manifestation" and is probably derived from the same root as *avatara*, which refers to the "incarnation" of a deity. Thus, in a Tantric sadhana (ritual enactment) associated with the *Heart Sutra,* the Buddha's entry into this samadhi is also described as representing the Buddha's entry into the womb of Prajnaparamita (cf. Donald Lopez, *Elaborations on Emptiness*, pp. 131–140). Elsewhere, the Buddha is described as residing in the vaginas of deities that represent the heart of all buddhas (cf. S. Bagchi, ed., *The Guhyasamaja Tantra*, p. 1). The reason a buddha enters this deepest of wombs is to show by example how to become a buddha.

While Prajnaparamita is sometimes personified as the goddess of the same name, more often this refers to the teaching that gave rise to Mahayana Buddhism. In its initial formulation in such scriptures as the *Ratnagunasancaya Gatha* and the *Perfection of Wisdom in Eight Thousand Lines*, this teaching focuses on the application of transcendent wisdom to the mundane understanding of the world as well as to the metaphysical understanding of the Abhidharma. This new approach, born of yogic insight rather than philosophical speculation, involved the dissolution of analytical categories without establishing any new ones to take their place. Thus, the teaching of Prajnaparamita could be characterized as Lao-tzu did the Tao, "The way that becomes a way / is not the Eternal Way / the name that becomes a name / is not the Eternal Name" (*Taoteching:* 1). Still, Lao-tzu proceeded to write eighty-one verses on what has no name. And the Buddha likewise spoke at great length on the Prajnaparamita.

This teaching developed quite naturally from the early Buddhist practice of the Three Skandhas, or Pillars: morality (*sila*), meditation (*dhyana*), and wisdom (*prajna*). With the introduction of the paramitas, or perfections, this threefold practice became sixfold: generosity (*dana*) now preceded morality, which was followed by forbearance (*kshanti*) and vigor (*virya*), after which came meditation and wisdom. According to some commentators, the first two paramitas of generosity and morality were the focus of lay practice and were intended to increase a person's *punya*, or merit, and the last two paramitas of meditation and wisdom were the focus of monastic practice and were intended to increase a person's *jnana*, or knowledge. The middle two paramitas of forbearance and vigor were the proper concern of all practitioners, lay and monastic, and were intended to increase a person's compassion and resolve.

Together, the paramitas represented a regimen of positive spiritual development, as opposed to earlier more proscriptive views of religious conduct, and a regimen that gave equal weight to lay practice. But what set the Six Paramitas apart from earlier conceptions of practice was their stress on the central role played by wisdom and the non-attachment that arises from its practice. Concerning the first paramita of generosity, Bodhid-harma once told his disciples, "Since what is real includes noth-ing worth begrudging, practitioners give their body, life, and property in charity, without regret, without the vanity of giver, gift, or recipient, and without bias or attachment. And to elim-inate impurity, they teach others, but without becoming attached to form" (Red Pine trans., *The Zen Teaching of Bodhid-harma*, p. 7). Thus, since the practice of the paramita of gen-erosity is based on an insight as to what is real, early Mahayana practitioners focused on wisdom as the key that makes the other paramitas effective. Wisdom is often described as the center of a five-petalled flower from which the fruit of buddhahood grows. In the *Perfection of Wisdom in Eight Thousand Lines*, the Buddha tells Ananda, "The paramita of wisdom incorporates the other five paramitas by means of practices that are based on all-embracing knowledge. Thus does the paramita of wisdom include the other five paramitas. The 'paramita of wisdom' is simply a synonym for the fruition of all six paramitas" (80–82).

Taken together, the paramitas are also likened to a boat that takes us across the sea of suffering. The paramita of generosity, according to this analogy, is the wood, light enough to float but not so light that it floats away. Thus bodhisattvas practice giving and renunciation but not so much that they have nothing left with which to work. The paramita of morality is the keel, deep enough to hold the boat upright but not so deep that it drags the shoals or holds it back. Thus bodhisattvas observe precepts but not so many that they have no freedom of choice. The para-mita of forbearance is the hull, wide enough to hold a deck but not so wide that it can't cut through waves. Thus bodhisattvas don't confront what opposes them but find the place of least resistance. The paramita of vigor is the mast, high enough to hold a sail but not so high that it tips the boat over. Thus bodhisattvas work hard but not so hard that they don't stop for tea. The paramita of meditation is the sail, flat enough to catch the wind of karma but not so flat that it holds no breeze or rips apart in a gale. Thus bodhisattvas still the mind but not so much that it withers and dies. And the paramita of wisdom is the helm, ingenious enough to give the boat direction but not so ingenious that it leads in circles. Thus bodhisattvas who practice the paramitas embark on the greatest of all voyages to the far shore of liberation.

Fa-tsang says, "The practice of prajna is of two kinds: shallow prajna, whereby persons are seen to be empty, and deep prajna, whereby dharmas are seen to be empty. Here, to note the difference, it describes prajna as deep. *Prajna* is the substance and means 'wisdom,' which is the spiritual awakening to the subtlest mysteries and the wondrous realization of the true source. *Paramita* is the function and means 'to reach the other shore,' which is to use this marvelous wisdom to transform sansara until one reaches completely beyond it to the realm of true emptiness."

Ching-mai says, "When bodhisattvas practice the Prajnaparamita, they do not think 'I am practicing the Prajnaparamita, or not practicing the Prajnaparamita, or not not practicing the Prajnaparamita. If bodhisattvas can practice like this, they can benefit countless beings. But they do not think there is any benefit. And why not? Because bodhisattvas do not perceive anything inside dharmas or outside dharmas."

Chih-shen says, "To practice means to proceed according to the principle of suchness thought after thought without stopping for a moment."

Huai-shen says, "This is the Mahayana practice of deep wisdom, not the Hinayana practice of superficial wisdom. It includes all practices that are not practiced and not clung to that never stop helping other beings. It is like when a magician performs magic in order to make people aware of illusion. This is why it is called 'the deep practice of Prajnaparamita.'"

Hui-ching says, "When a person is asleep, they might dream they're in a boat, that they're crossing a river and reaching the other shore. Then they suddenly wake up at home, and the river and the person in the boat are gone. When bodhisattvas cultivate the Way, they understand that both people and dharmas are empty. And after approaching the end of the path and gaining the forbearance of birthlessness, they realize that the person who cultivates and the path they cultivate are nothing but a dream or illusion."

Deva says, "Prajnaparamita is the name of the dharma-kaya, the body that is neither born nor destroyed, that neither comes nor goes, that has the dimensions of emptiness, that is changeless, that fills the entire universe and includes all things and yet fits inside a mustard seed or a mote of dust, and for which metaphors fail."

3. LOOKED UPON THE FIVE SKANDHAS:
vyaavalokayati sma panca skandhas 照見五蘊

The verb *avaloka* means "to look (down) upon," and *vya* is an emphatic. Hence, the literal meaning of *vya-avaloka-yati* is "to look down upon intently." Thus, Avalokiteshvara practices the practice for which he was named, looking down from above, and perhaps thereby betrays an association with the hill gods of ancient India, if not with the deva Santushita at the summit of Mount Sumeru.

In the earliest texts that deal with meditation, practitioners are advised to begin by focusing their attention on four subjects (*catvari smirti-upasthanani*): form, sensations, mind, and finally dharmas, the constructs of the mind that such sects as the Sarvastivadins maintained were the underlying substance of reality. This fourfold scheme was probably an earlier variation of the Five Skandhas, which also began with form and sensation but which then divided mind into perception, memory, and consciousness. It didn't bother with dharmas, because they were subsumed under the various skandhas.

The reason Buddhists focused on the Four Smirti Upasthanas or the Five Skandhas is that they provide everything we need in our spiritual explorations. They are not only equivalent to what we normally think of as our selves; they are equivalent to the entire universe, as we experience it. They include all of creation. This is what Avalokiteshvara looks down upon. The Greek philosopher Archimedes once claimed he could move the world if he had a place to stand and a long enough lever. Avalokiteshvara has found such a place and such a lever.

The Western inquiry into reality generally follows the Cartesian dictum "I think, therefore I am." The Five Skandhas are an early example of the Buddhist solution to the same sort of self-reflection. But instead of taking the Archimedean standpoint vis-à-vis an external world, the Buddhist analysis never goes beyond our immediate experience. And as a result of reflecting on this experience, Buddhists conclude: "I am aware, therefore I neither am nor am not." Thus, by taking his stand on the emptiness of self-existence, Avalokiteshvara uses the lever of prajna to move the world of the skandhas.

The Sanskrit word *skandha* refers to the trunk of a tree, and I think the trunk of a banyan, or *Ficus indica*, might have been what the Buddha had in mind when he started using this term. The banyan is one of the world's most unusual trees. It begins as an aerial root that descends from a seed dropped by a bird in the canopy of another tree, such as a palm. After the seed sprouts, its root descends until it reaches the ground, and once established, it strangles its host. As it continues to grow, its branches put forth their own aerial roots, and these, in turn, form additional trunks. In the course of a hundred years, the original trunk becomes impossible to distinguish among the grove of roots that develop into trunks. In Sri Lanka, there is a banyan that has more than 350 major trunks and 3,000 minor ones and that forms its own forest. Thus, the banyan is called "the tree that walks."

The Buddha frequently sought shelter within the wide,

outstretched root structure of such trees. And we know from Vatsyayana's commentary on the aphorisms of Akshapada in the *Nyaya Sutras* (II: 1087) that from a distance a skandha was sometimes mistaken for a human being. Hence, it is not surprising that the Buddha chose a word like this to refer to this host-strangling-root that looks like a person. But instead of seeing the individual as a single skandha, the Buddha saw five skandhas, as he considered a person's experience of the world from five different perspectives. Whether this fivefold analysis originated with Shakyamuni or he learned about it from someone else is unknown. The Jains also used the word *skandha* for any whole object, including the individual. But the Buddha appears to have been alone in analyzing the individual and the individual's experience of reality from five points of view. The fact that he often had to explain what he meant by the Five Skandhas suggests they represented a form of analysis not widely known, even to the disciples of other teachers.

Before considering what the Five Skandhas include, I should note that translators have generally settled on "aggregate" as their preferred rendering of this term in English. Given the word's multiple meanings, such a translation is possible, though, I suggest, inappropriate in this context. For it emphasizes a derivative meaning that distorts the word's basic frame of reference. This derivative meaning was the one chosen by Vasubandhu in his *Abhidharmakoshabhasaya*, and it has been used ever since by commentators cognizant of this classic work on the Abhidharma. However, *skandha* refers to a tree trunk or a pillar made from a tree trunk and not a pile of wood. I will not belabor the point and only hope future translators and commentators will continue to explore this issue.

In his use of the word *skandha*, the Buddha views the universe of our awareness as supported by these five trunks or pillars, or as consisting of these five aspects, which are separate in name only, and each of which exhausts everything of which we are aware from a different point of view. I have sometimes thought of them as overlays in an anatomy textbook: the skin, the musculature, the skeleton, the circulatory system, and the nervous system, to name only five. But this, of course, is only an analogy and should not be misconstrued as referring to an actual body or an individual self. Rather they represent a system of analysis designed to find our actual bodies or individual selves.

The first skandha in this analysis of our awareness is *rupa*, or form. *Rupa* is not the material world. It is simply the outside world, in contrast to what we presume is an inside world. Thus, the word *rupa* does not actually refer to a concrete object but to the appearance of an object. Form is like a mask that cannot be removed without revealing its own illusory identity. Such a mask might be worn by a table or a sunset or a number or a coin (the rupee), or a universe. Whether such things are real is not relevant. The important thing is that they make up a presumed outside to a presumed inside.

In the Buddha's system of analysis, the skandha of form includes not only appearances but also the means by which those appearances are apprehended. Thus, form is not an objective category but a subjective one extrapolated from a person's own experience and beyond which it has little, if any, meaning. In order to substantiate the existence of an external world, and thus to prove the existence of an inner one, a means is needed whereby that external world can be known. The Buddhist definition of form thus includes the powers of the eyes, the ears, the nose, the tongue, and the skin as well as the domains in which they function: sight, sound, smell, taste, and feeling. Hence rupa is not limited to what we normally think of as our body; it includes the sun and the wind and the bamboo outside the window and the window and whatever else we might find in and through the five senses.

To provide some members of his audience with a more accessible entrance into this universe of form, the Buddha further analyzed these powers and domains as representing different combinations of the Four Elements: earth (solidity), water (moisture), fire (heat), and wind (motion). These were already part of general discourse in the Buddha's day, and his inclusion of them was more like sugar-coating for the materialist members of his audience. But while the materialists of ancient India also included the element of space (*akasha*) in their five-element view of the universe, the Buddha omitted this as having no relevance for what was basically a phenomenological approach. Essentially, form is a conceptual category established in order to give meaning to mind. Form does not represent a separate reality outside of mind, merely a stage on which to proceed with the analysis.

Altogether, there are ten kinds of form, or fourteen, if the four elements are included as a subcategory. As noted, the ten include the five powers of sensation and their five respective domains. Several centuries after the Buddha's Nirvana, some Abhidharma schools, notably the Sarvastivadins, added an eleventh category for forms that were presumed to exist but whose existence could not be verified by the five senses. For the Sarvastivadins this category was primarily intended to allow the existence of past and future dharmas. However, it was not accepted by other schools, in particular the Darshtantikas. This category and the difference of opinion regarding its validity are worth noting because the position of the Darshtantikas, and later that of the Sautrantikas, was to treat all dharmas, including this eleventh kind of form, as so many ripples in the stream of consciousness and empty of any self-existence. This was in stark contrast to the Sarvastivadins, who held that all dharmas were essentially real. Thus, the teaching of the *Heart Sutra* did not simply fall out of the sky but more likely evolved out of such conflicts as this over the status of form (cf. "On the Possibility of a Nonexistent Object of Consciousness: Sarvastivadin and Darshtantika Theories" by Collett Cox in the *Journal of the International Association of Buddhist Studies*, vol. 11, no. 1, 1988).

In any case, these various kinds of form were thought to account for our experience of an external world. Thus, with the backdrop of an outside established, the Buddha continued with an analysis of the inside, which he divided into four additional skandhas. These were apparently developed from the second half of an earlier bipartite division of reality into *nama-rupa*. According to this twofold scheme, *rupa*, or form, refers to the things we know, namely the outside world, while *nama*, or name, refers to the means by which we know the things we know, namely the inside world. From a Western perspective, this might be interpreted as a division into matter and mind, but it was more of a division into objective mind and subjective mind.

In turning his attention to *nama*, the Buddha began his analysis of "subjective mind" with sensation, or *vedana*, and made this the second skandha. The word *vedana* was derived from *vid*, meaning "to know" or "to experience," and was used by Buddhists to refer to our evaluation of form. Once one establishes the existence of form, sensation necessarily follows as the interface between *nama* and *rupa*, between inner mind and outer mind. Although to call it an interface does not mean it is separate. None of the skandhas are separate in any sense other than as analytical constructs. They merely represent different ways of looking at the same experience. The skandha of sensation looks at our experience as a process of evaluation. This is not the same as sensory input but rather the evaluation of input, which the Buddha rarely described in any more detail than positive, negative, or neutral. For the most part, our experiences are neutral and ignored. But certain experiences appear to satisfy a need or pose a danger and are classified accordingly. As we walk through a forest our eyes take in countless appearances, but we quickly focus on a snake or a wildflower or some object that might affect our continued existence. Thus, Buddhists do not understand sensation as the passive collection of data from an outside world but as the active sorting and grading of appearances and their transformation into objects according to categories supplied by the third skandha.

The third skandha is perception, or *sanjna*. Like sensation, perception was also included as a subcategory of the earlier concept of *nama*. The word *sanjna* is derived from *san* (together) and *jna* (to know) and refers to our experience as a kaleidoscope of conceptual combinations. Without the skandha of perception, our sensations cannot be classified as positive, negative, or neutral. Perception supplies the framework that allows us to make such judgments as well as the framework that allows us to objectify or subjectify our experience. It also supplies the means that allow us to manipulate our sensations, so that we see what we want to see and don't see what we don't want to see. Thus, sensation is dependent not only on the skandha of form but also on the skandha of perception. And likewise, the skandha of perception is dependent on sensation as well as the fourth skandha, which is the source of its seemingly never-ending supply of conceptual constructs.

The fourth skandha is *sanskara*, which I have translated as "memory," and which replaced both volition (*cetana*) and attention (*manasikara*) as subcategories of *nama*. The word *sanskara* is derived from a combination of *san* (together) and *kri* (to make). Thus, it means "put together" and refers to those things we have "put together" that have a direct bearing on the way we think or perceive. In the past this term has often been translated as "impulse," "volition," "predisposition," or "mental conformation." But each of these renderings involves certain limitations and distortions. For example, "volition" suggests a separate will tantamount to a self, and "impulse" implies the lack of any will or self. "Predisposition" comes closer but does not necessarily establish a connection with past actions. And such invented terms as "mental conformation" are simply too bizarre to have much use outside academic circles, very small academic circles. What this term basically refers to is our karmic genome, the repository of all that we have previously intended, whether expressed in the form of words, deeds, or thoughts. Thus, *sanskara* embraces all the ways we have dealt with what we have experienced in the past and that are available to us as ways to deal with what we find in the present. Among the meanings for *sanskara* listed by Monier-Williams is "the faculty of memory, mental impression or recollection, impression on the mind of acts done in a former state of existence … the reproductive imagination … a mental conformation or creation of the mind (such as that of the external world, regarded by it as real, though actually non-existent" (*Sanskrit–English Dictionary*, p. 1120).

Under the skandha of *sanskara*, the Sarvastivadins listed fifty-two kinds of habitual behavior patterns, such as intelligence, belief, shame, confidence, indolence, pride, anger, envy, sloth, repentance, doubt, anything that might provide us with a prefabricated set of guidelines from the past with which to perceive and deal with the world, both inside and outside, as we experience it in the present. Thus, the skandha of memory supplies the templates that perception applies to sensations and form.

And how do we know this? Because we are conscious of it. Thus, the fifth and final skandha is consciousness (*vijnana*). The *vi* in *vijnana* means "to divide." Thus, just as *san-jna* emphasizes knowledge that results from combination, *vi-jna* emphasizes knowledge that results from separation, separation of subject from object and one object from another. Hence, *vijnana* is often translated as "discrimination." In terms of the skandhas, *vijnana* refers to the faculty of the mind in general, the ability to be aware, aware of anything, but always something—form, sensations, perceptions, memories, and, of course, a "self." It is the least discussed or analyzed of the skandhas because to discuss or analyze consciousness would be like the hand trying to grab itself. In the Abhidharma matrices that divide the other skandhas into various subcategories, consciousness is simply consciousness.

But if we stop to consider these five pillars that support our awareness, it becomes clear that the *Heart Sutra* presents them to us backward in order to make them easier to grasp for those whose understanding of reality begins with the material world. In terms of the world as we actually experience it, we begin with the skandha of consciousness and then extrapolate the memory of previous states of consciousness from which we then extrapolate perceptions from which we extrapolate sensations from which we extrapolate an objectified world of form.

Basically the skandhas represent an attempt to exhaust the possible paths we might take in our search for a self, for something permanent or pure or separate in the undifferentiated flux of experience. They are five ways of considering our world and looking for something we can call our own. This is why Avalokiteshvara looks upon the Five Skandhas. The Five Skandhas are the limit of reality. If we are going to find anything real, this is where we are going to find it. But no matter how often or how long or how intently we search through the skandhas, we come up empty-handed. Thus, the skandha of form is often compared to foam, because it cannot be grasped; the skandha of sensation to a bubble, because it lasts but an instant; the skandha of perception to a mirage, because it only appears to exist;the skandha of memory to a banana tree, because it has no core; and the skandha of consciousness to an illusion, because it is a well-concealed deception. And yet the skandhas are not separate from what is real.

In the *Samyukt Agama*, the Buddha asks the ascetic Shrenika Vatsagotra if the Tathagata (another name for a buddha) is the same as the skandhas, and Shrenika says, "No, Bhagavan." Again the Buddha asks if the Tathagata is separate from the skandhas, and again Shrenika answers, "No, Bhagavan." The Buddha then asks if the Tathagata is inside the skandhas. Again Shrenika answers, "No, Bhagavan." The Buddha then asks if the skandhas are inside the Tathagata. Once more Shrenika says, "No, Bhagavan." Finally the Buddha asks if the Tathagata is not the skandhas, to which Shrenika answers, "No, Bhagavan" (105). Likewise, in the *Perfection of Wisdom in Eight Thousand Lines*, the Buddha says that enlightenment is neither inside the skandhas nor outside them, nor both inside and outside them, nor other than the skandhas (I: 9).

When the early Sarvastivadin Abhidharma masters laid out their matrices of reality, they listed all but three of their seventy-five dharmas under these five categories. Only space and two kinds of nirvana were considered outside their reach. Thus, it is important to keep in mind that the skandhas include everything we think of as real, and not just our physical body. They include five possible bodies, each of which is limited in extent only by our awareness and our willingness and ability to differentiate.

Chen-k'o says, "The Five Skandhas are the root of the ten-thousand forms of suffering and the basis of the thousand calamities. Because beings don't yet realize they are empty, they are entangled and ensnared by them."

Ching-chueh says, "The *Madhyamaka-karika* says, 'What I call "me" is the combination of the Five Skandhas, not something that is fixed. It is like when we put posts and beams together to make a house. If we take away the posts and beams, there is no house.' Also, inside a house that has been dark for a thousand years, a person doesn't realize there are jewels or sense the presence of demons and thieves. But once a lamp is lit, the darkness vanishes, and everything becomes clear. Thus, precious stones appear when the water is clear, and the moon shines bright when the clouds part."

Conze says, "The first step towards wisdom consists in getting the *skandhas* into view. This requires considerable knowledge, practice and skill, but it is the indispensable basis for all that follows" (*Buddhist Wisdom Books*, p. 79).

4. AND SEEING THEY WERE EMPTY OF SELF-EXISTENCE:
tansh ca svabhava shunyan pashyati sma 皆空(度一切苦厄)

The verb here is *pashyati*, which means "to see." In the Buddha's day, a person who saw what others did not see was called a *pashyaka*, or seer. Avalokiteshvara's seeing is deep seeing. It is like seeing into the structure of the universe, but even deeper.

Applying a similar perspective in the search for our selves,

George Leonard asks, "Of what is the body made? It is made of emptiness and rhythm. At the ultimate heart of the body, at the heart of the world, there is no solidity ... there is only the dance" (*The Silent Pulse*, p. 34). This, however, is still the "seeing" of physics, which is limited by its focus on the "physical" world. Avalokiteshvara's perspective is incomparably wider and deeper, for it takes in the world of mind as well as matter. Still, he, too, sees the emptiness of the elements into which early Buddhists divided reality. This was not a new discovery on Avalokiteshvara's part. It was part of the Buddha's earliest teaching. But what was new, at least as far as the Sarvastivadins were concerned, was that these elements were not simply declared to be empty but to be empty of *sva-bhava* or "self-existence."

This "self" (*sva*) whose existence (*bhava*) was maintained by some Buddhists was more generalized in its application than "ego" (*atman*) and referred not only to beings but to any inherent substance that could be identified as existing in time or space as a permanent or independent entity. Thus, the term *sva-bhava* is somewhat redundant, implying a "self-existing existence." From the point of view of Mahayana Buddhism, this is the greatest of all delusions, the belief that something exists. Upon close analysis, nothing exists by itself. Any given entity can only be defined in terms of other entities in time, space, or mind. And these in turn can only be defined in terms of other entities, and so on *ad infinitum*. Thus, nothing exists by itself, and nothing exists as itself. There is no such thing as a self.

Here, Avalokiteshvara looks at the skandhas and sees that they are empty, or *shunya*. The Sanskrit word *shunya* means "hollow," "void," or "zero." What is hollow, void, or zero is the existence of a self. But if there is no self-existence, there is also no non-existence. According to Mahayana Buddhism, this is the second greatest of all delusions, the belief that nothing exists. Emptiness does not mean nothingness. It simply means the absence of the erroneous distinctions that divide one entity from another, one being from another being, one thought from another thought. Emptiness is not nothing, it's everything, everything at once. This is what Avalokiteshvara sees.

After this line, the Chinese translations of Kumarajiva, Hsuan-tsang, and Yi-ching interpolate the line "and was healed from all suffering" (*tu yi-ch'ieh k'u-o*). Most likely they noted the occurrence of this phrase near the end of the sutra in line 33 and decided a second occurrence near the beginning would help emphasize the point that emptiness is not nothingness but what liberates us from suffering. No other Chinese translation, however, follows suit. Nor has any Sanskrit copy been found that contains this line.

Conze says, "Etymologically, *shunya* (empty) conveys the idea that something, which looks like something much, is really nothing. From outside there appears to be a lot, but there is really nothing behind. A 'swelled' head, as we know, is an 'empty' head" (*Buddhist Wisdom Books*, p. 80).

Fa-tsang says, "Although the absolute and provisional are both submerged, their two truths are permanently present. Although emptiness and existence are both denied, their one meaning shines forever. True emptiness has never not existed, but by means of existence it is distinguished from emptiness.

Illusory existence has been empty from time without beginning, but by means of emptiness it is seen as existing. Because existence is an empty existence, it does not exist. And because emptiness is an existent emptiness, it is not empty. Emptiness which is not empty, does not stop being empty. And existence which does not exist, exists but not forever."

Chen-k'o says, "This line is the heart of this sutra. Ordinary people are deluded and don't realize this body is a temporary combination of the Four Elements and consider it real. Thus, they hear about life and are pleased. They hear about death and are distressed. They don't have any idea that by viewing this body as the Four Elements, they can't find anyone who is born or dies. If the body is like this, then so is the mind. Its delusions, reasonings, and shadows are nothing but a combination of the four other skandhas. But by viewing the mind as the four skandhas, they also can't find anyone who suffers."

Hui-ching says, "If the skandhas exist, then suffering isn't empty. But once someone understands that the skandhas are empty, what does suffering have to rest on? For example, when the wind blows against water, it creates bubbles. As long as they're bubbles, they aren't water. But when bubbles disperse and become water, they aren't bubbles. Bubbles represent beings, and water represents our buddha nature."

Lao-tzu says, "The reason we have suffering / is because we have a body / if we didn't have a body / we wouldn't have suffering" (13).

5. SAID, "HERE, SHARIPUTRA: *iha shariputra* 舍利子

The emphatic *iha* (here) is often omitted by translators but is one of the most important words in the sutra. *Iha* is the Zen master's shout, the poke in the ribs, the cup of tea. This was the basis of the fifth point of contention at Buddhism's Third Council, held in 267 B.C., or one hundred and sixteen years after the Buddha's Nirvana. This council was convened by King Ashoka in Pataliputra (modern Patna), and is said to have concerned itself with five issues raised by the monk Mahadeva. The first four concerned the status of the *arhan*, the hero of the shravaka tradition: Was an arhan still subject to sexual desire, was an arhan still subject to ignorance, was an arhan still subject to doubt, and was an arhan still subject to further instruction? The fifth issue was whether a person could become enlightened by an exclamation or sudden sound. As the questions raised by Mahadeva were all answered in the affirmative, this essentially lowered the status of the arhan and opened up the possibility of enlightenment outside the confines of monastic practice. Thus, this council is often seen (by the Mahayana) as marking the beginning of the split into the Hinayana and Mahayana traditions.

Thus, with "here" Avalokiteshvara opens the door to the Great Path of the Mahayana. Right here, right now, in the light of Prajnaparamita, he looks at the skandhas that the Sarvastivadins considered real and sees the absence of anything permanent, anything pure, anything separate, anything complete unto itself. And he conveys this realization to the disciple of the Buddha best known for his analysis of the self-existence of the skandhas. Thus, Avalokiteshvara gives the skandhas a name, the name Shariputra.

Unlike Avalokiteshvara, we know a great deal about Shariputra. In ancient India, children often received two names, one from each parent. Thus, Shariputra was sometimes referred to as *Upa-tishya*, "child of Tishya," after his father, who was a Brahman priest. But more often he was called *Shari-putra*, "son of Shari," after his mother, whose eyes were said to resemble those of the *shari*, or Indian myna (*Gracula religiosa*). As a child Shariputra was expected to follow in his father's footsteps, and as a youth he was known for his knowledge of Brahman scriptures and his skill in debating points of doctrine, which he often did with his boyhood friend, Maudgalyayana. *Maudgaly-ayana*, the "offspring of Maudgali," the "crow," was also named for his mother, and these two sons of bird-eyed women lived in the neighboring villages of Nalaka and Kolita. Their two families had been linked with one another for seven generations, and both boys were not only born on the same day, they were also conceived on the same day.

As young men Shariputra and Maudgalyayana often traveled together to Rajgir, the nearby capital of the kingdom of Magadha, to attend important festivals. During one such occasion, they both came to the realization that their lives of pleasure were doomed to end, and they vowed to attain deliverance from such transient existence. After exchanging their white robes for rags, the two friends sought out Sanjaya, the leader of a group of sophists. They were at first attracted by his arguments, but the two men soon exhausted the depths of Sanjaya's teachings. And when they realized they had nothing more to learn from him, they wandered off in search of someone else who could teach them how to escape the sufferings of this life and the next. After visiting teachers throughout Northern India without success, they finally found themselves back in Rajgir and decided to part company for a while. But first they made a pact that whichever of them found the path to liberation would tell the other.

Not long afterward, Shariputra decided to revisit his old teacher, Sanjaya. And on his way there, he saw Ashvajit making his morning rounds begging in the city. Ashvajit was Shakyamuni's cousin and also one of his first five disciples. Impressed with Ashvajit's demeanor, Shariputra asked him who his teacher was and what teaching he followed. Ashvajit replied that Shakyamuni was his teacher. As for what teaching he followed, he would only say, "Of what arises from causes / the Buddha shows how it begins / and also how it ceases / thus does the Great Recluse instruct." This subsequently became one of the most widely quoted summaries of the Buddha's teaching in India, and upon hearing it, Shariputra realized the first of the four stages of attainment known as "reaching the river," the river of impermanence.

Shariputra was so overwhelmed, he went at once to find his friend Maudgalyayana, who also experienced the same level of realization upon hearing the same verse. Both men then decided to become disciples of the Buddha, but Shariputra suggested they first tell their former teacher and ask him to join them. Sanjaya, however, was unwilling to become the disciple of another man. And so Shariputra and Maudgalyayana left to find the

74 THE HEART SUTRA

Buddha, taking with them five hundred of Sanjaya's disciples.

When the Buddha saw the two men and their entourage approaching, he told his disciples that these two would become his two chief disciples. He ordained them and within a week Maudgalyayana had reached the fourth and final stage of an arhan, or one who is free of passion and destined for no further rebirth. After another week, Shariputra also reached the birthless state. It was said it took him a week longer because he thought through the Buddha's teachings in greater detail. Thus, during the Buddha's lifetime, Maudgalyayana was ranked first among the Buddha's disciples in terms of spiritual powers, and Shariputra was ranked first in terms of wisdom. In statues or paintings, Shariputra always stands on the Buddha's right, and Maudgalyayana on the Buddha's left. During the Buddha's ministry, Shariputra was also his chief assistant and occasionally took his place in preaching the Dharma.

After forty-some years of wandering with his teacher across the floodplain of the Ganges, Shariputra finally returned home to teach his mother. But while he was there, he became ill and died. This was in the spring of 383 B.C., six months before the Buddha entered Nirvana. In 1851, Shariputra's relics, along with those of his friend Maudgalyayana, were discovered in a stupa excavated by Alexander Cunningham at Sanchi, near Bhopal in Central India. In Chapter Three of the *Lotus Sutra*, the Buddha predicted Shariputra would forsake the goal of nirvana and turn instead to the bodhisattva path and eventually become the buddha Padmaprabha. With this in mind, the *Heart Sutra* can be read as his first step in his new career.

Chih-hsu says, "If you want to know how to get down the mountain, you need to ask someone coming up. Thus, we are given the example of someone who has successfully examined their mind."

6. FORM IS EMPTINESS, EMPTINESS IS FORM:
rupan shunyata shunyataiva rupan 色即是空，空即是色

Buddhist commentators distinguish five kinds of emptiness: the emptiness of pre-existence, the emptiness of post-existence, the emptiness of non-existence, the emptiness of mutual exclusion, and the emptiness of self-existence. Avalokiteshvara is referring to this last form of emptiness.

There are many ways of viewing this statement. From a purely historical point of view, the first part was aimed at the Sarvastivadins, who believed such dharmas as form were self-existent, and the second part was aimed at the Sautrantikas, who believed that the skandha of consciousness was self-existent. Having seen that all five skandhas are empty of anything self-existent, Avalokiteshvara turns from the Hinayana interpretation of emptiness, which holds that there is some aspect of certain dharmas that persists over time, to that of the Mahayana.

That form is empty was one of the Buddha's earliest and most frequent pronouncements. But in the light of Prajnaparamita, form is not simply empty, it is so completely empty, it is emptiness itself, which turns out to be the same as form itself.

The logic of this, which has become the most famous statement in Mahayana Buddhism, goes like this: Form, or any other

entity of the mind, is defined by the mind and exists only
because we claim it exists. The only thing that exists, in this case,
is our definition of form. Form itself is empty of anything that
could be called self-existent. Whatever we use to define form, it
is dependent on something else. Thus, the essential nature of
form is emptiness. But emptiness is simply another name for
reality—not just a part of reality, for reality has no parts, but all
of reality—though neither can reality be considered to be a
whole. The essential nature of reality is that it is indivisible, or
empty of anything self-existent. But if form is equivalent to
emptiness, or the indivisible fabric of reality, then emptiness
must also be equivalent to form. Thus, Avalokiteshvara goes
beyond the understanding of early Buddhists, who understood
that form is empty, and surprises Shariputra with the statement
"emptiness is form." Avalokiteshvara turns Shariputra's understanding of the Abhidharma upside-down and tells him that in
the light of wisdom the seamless fabric of reality is equivalent to
any attempt to separate reality into parts, including parts, such
as form, that themselves are attempts to account for all of reality, as we experience it. The absence of anything self-existent is
the true nature of all that we experience, however distorted that
experience might be by the matrix of our minds. But it is also the
true nature of reality.

This, then, is the hub around which this sutra turns, the equation that puts an end to the dualistic conception of reality. The
problem that arises when we reflect on our experience is that
we reflect on our experience. We think, therefore we are. And
once we are, we are in trouble, forever divided by what we use to

define our existence. In analyzing the elements of this particular definition of self-existence, namely the Five Skandhas, Avalokiteshvara sees that they are empty of anything permanent, pure, or inherent; they are empty of anything real. They are empty as a group, and they are empty individually. They are so completely empty, we might be tempted to say that they do not exist. But we can't say that they do not exist, because they exist as delusions. And we can't say they do not not exist, because they are completely empty. Thus, as used by Avalokiteshvara, and by Mahayana Buddhists in general, the word "emptiness" does not mean nothingness. It is a double negative that stops short of establishing a positive. Emptiness means indivisibility.

Something that is empty of self-existence is inseparable from everything else, including emptiness. All separations are delusions. But if each of the skandhas is one with emptiness, and emptiness is one with each of the skandhas, then everything occupies the same indivisible space, which is emptiness, and the same indivisible time, which is also emptiness, and the same indivisible mind, which is emptiness again. Everything is empty, and empty is everything. Avalokiteshvara denies all views regarding the skandhas that would regard any of them as real by telling us that "form is emptiness." But he also denies all views that would regard any of them as annihilated by telling us that "emptiness is form." Neither do the skandhas exist, nor do they not exist. What we are left with is a koan: "form is emptiness and emptiness is form."

Ching-chueh says, "According to the *Perfection of Wisdom in Twenty-five Thousand Lines*, 'Form is emptiness. Form does not annihilate emptiness.' Hence, those who realize the Way do not use emptiness to perceive form, for they know that form essentially is not form. Nor do they use form to perceive emptiness, for they know that essentially emptiness is not emptiness."

Pao-t'ung says, "Form and emptiness are the same. From the buddhas above down to the smallest insect below, every creature is basically empty. This form cannot be seen by the eyes. Only true emptiness can see it. And this form cannot be heard by the ears. Only true emptiness can hear it. The myriad things we know and feel all depend on our six senses. But form and emptiness are not separate."

Chen-k'o says, "In the distance, form includes the Great Void, heaven and earth, mountains and rivers and forests. Nearby, it includes this body of flesh and blood that appears before us. Regardless of whether it's large or small, if it can be perceived, it's called 'form.'"

Ming-k'uang says, "Form and the mind are not two different dharmas. And how so? The mind is not inside or outside or somewhere in between. It extends everywhere. It's like space."

Hui-ching says, "Followers of lesser paths use emptiness to eliminate form, unaware that emptiness is their own mind. But if the mind sees emptiness, then emptiness becomes an object and an obstruction. And an obstruction is another name for 'form.' But bodhisattvas understand the nature of form is simply emptiness, not form cancels emptiness, and not formlessness is emptiness, and not emptiness depends on insight, and not emptiness is due to no mind, and not emptiness means cutting off dharmas."

Yin-shun says, "Most people don't understand this. They think that 'emptiness' means 'nothing' and that it can't produce everything that exists. They don't realize that if dharmas weren't empty, no dharmas would ever appear, that what exists would always exist and what doesn't exist would never exist. But dharmas aren't like that. Those that exist can change, then they don't exist. And those that don't exist can appear to exist as the result of causes and conditions. The birth and destruction, the existence and non-existence of dharmas is entirely dependent on their lack of self-existence and their fundamental emptiness. Thus, Nagarjuna said, 'Because of emptiness, all things are possible.'"

Conze says, "The infinitely Far-away is not only near, but it is infinitely near. It is nowhere, and nowhere it is not. This is the mystical identity of opposites. Nirvana is the same as the world. It is not only 'in' and 'with you,' but you are nothing but it" (*Buddhist Wisdom Books*, p. 83).

7. EMPTINESS IS NOT SEPARATE FROM FORM, FORM IS NOT SEPARATE FROM EMPTINESS: *rupan na prithak shunyata sunyataya na prithag rupan* 色不異空 , 空不異色

In considering this relationship, Avalokiteshvara realizes that it only works because form and emptiness are inseparable. Thus, he advances their equation by eliminating the possibility that form and emptiness overlap but do not completely coincide. Not only are they identical, they are not different. Although two entities might be the same under certain conditions, it is still possible that under other conditions they differ. This statement eliminates that possibility. There are no conditions under which form is different from emptiness or emptiness is different from form. Emptiness and form are closer than inseparable; they are essentially indistinguishable. Thus, because of its relationship with emptiness, form is neither permanent nor impermanent. Form cannot be permanent because it is emptiness. And form cannot be impermanent because it is emptiness. The same holds for form and suffering or form and the presence of a self.

Chen-k'o says, "As for seeing that the Five Skandhas are empty, this is not an emptiness separate from the skandhas but the emptiness of the skandhas. The emptiness realized by Ava-lokiteshvara is not the one-sided emptiness of the Lesser Path and not an emptiness of senselessness or an emptiness of anni-hilation. It is simply the emptiness that is form. Since form can be emptiness, emptiness can be form. Thus, it says 'form is not separate from emptiness and emptiness is not separate from form.'"

Hui-chung says, "People misapprehend their own mind and see form as something outside their mind. They don't know that form exists because of their mind. And where could form come from, if not from their mind? Thus, it says, 'Form is not separate from emptiness.' People turn their backs on their mind and grab hold of dharmas and think emptiness is something outside their mind. They don't know that emptiness arises from their mind. All they need to do is awaken to their own mind. There is no emptiness to find. Emptiness and form are not separate. Thus, it says, 'emptiness is not separate from form.'"

Chih-shen says, "Inside emptiness there is no form. Outside form there is no emptiness. Emptiness and form are one suchness. Thus they are not separate."

Ching-chueh says, "According to Nagarjuna, 'Form illuminates emptiness. Without form there is no emptiness. And emptiness illuminates form. Without emptiness there is no form. Emptiness and form share the same nature.' Hence, they are said to be "not separate." This is the teaching of the One Path."

Te-ch'ing says, "The statement 'form is not separate from emptiness' destroys the ordinary person's view of permanence. This is because ordinary people think that only their material body is real. And because they consider it permanent, they make hundred-year plans and don't realize their body is an empty fiction and subject to the ceaseless changes of birth, old age, illness, and death. But even when it reaches old age and death and finally becomes impermanent and turns out to be empty, this is still the emptiness of origination and cessation and not yet the final truth. Consequently, the illusory forms of the Four Elements are basically no different from true emptiness. But ordinary people don't know this. Thus, it says, 'form is not separate from emptiness.' This means that the physical body is basically not different from true emptiness.

"As for the statement 'emptiness is not separate from form,' this statement destroys the view of annihilation held by followers of the Lesser Path and members of other sects. Although members of other sects cultivate, they remain unaware that their body comes from karma and karma comes from the mind, and they go around life after life without stop. And because they don't understand the principle of retribution that occurs from one lifetime to the next due to cause and effect, they think that after someone dies, their pure breath returns to heaven and their coarse breath returns to earth, and their true spirit returns to the Great Void. But if their essence returns to the Great Void, then there would be no retribution, and doing good would be useless, and doing evil would have its advantage. And if their essence returns to the Great Void, all their good and evil deeds would leave no traces, which would amount to nihilism. Would that not be unfortunate?

"Although followers of the Lesser Path use the teachings of the Buddha in their practice, because they don't understand that the world is nothing but mind and the myriad dharmas are nothing but ideas, they don't realize that life and death are illusions, and they think the forms of the Three Realms really exist. Thus, they regard the world as a prison and birth as shackles. They don't give rise to the thought of saving others but sink into emptiness and quietude and drown in the stillness of nirvana. Thus it says, 'emptiness is not separate from form.' The true emptiness of prajna is like a huge round mirror, and every illusory form is like an image in the mirror. Once you know that images don't exist apart from the mirror, you know 'emptiness is not separate from form.'"

8. WHATEVER IS FORM IS EMPTINESS, WHATEVER IS EMPTINESS IS FORM: *yad rupan sa shunyata ya shunyata tad rupan* 是色彼空，是空彼色

This completes the comparison of form and emptiness and carries their mutual identification to its logical conclusion by allowing for variations in our definitions of form or emptiness. Regardless of how we might conceive of form or emptiness, they are identical. In viewing such conceptual categories as form, Avalokiteshvara sees that they can only be established in terms of emptiness. All other terms, such as those that would discriminate an individual entity as permanent, unique, or real, turn out to be inadequate to the task. And emptiness can only be established in terms of categories that are *a priori* empty. Whatever we might consider emptiness to be, it is identical to whatever conceptual category we might dream up, in this case the skandha of form.

The existence of form is not denied, nor its non-existence. It exists as a category of analysis. But every analysis involves the use of terms that are essentially the same. For example, in mathematics, if we are actually able to write the perfect formula and establish the coefficient of x and y as 1, that is, if any given movement on the x axis is reflected by an equal movement on the y axis, not only are they equal, their original differentiation as x and y must be a mistake. Thus, however we define form or emptiness, they are one and the same in all times and in all places and under all conditions.

Fa-tsang says, "Before they enter nirvana, followers of lesser paths see the skandhas as devoid of a self and dharmas as empty. They look on the emptiness of the skandhas as referring to the absence of a self in the skandhas and not to the skandhas themselves being empty. Thus, for them, the skandhas are different from emptiness. But now they are told that the self-existence of the skandhas is essentially empty, which is not the same. Thus, it says 'form is not separate from emptiness' and so on. Also, according to their understanding of what happens after they enter nirvana, the body and knowledge both disappear into emptiness devoid of form. Thus, for these followers of lesser paths, form is not emptiness. Only when form ceases to exist is there emptiness. But now they are told that it is not so, that 'form is emptiness' and not 'form cancels emptiness.' Thus, this is in answer to the doubts of shravakas and pratyeka-buddhas.

"Bodhisattvas also have doubts. First, they wonder if form is different from emptiness and grasp an emptiness external to form. To put an end to this doubt, they are now told 'form is not separate from emptiness.' Second, they wonder if emptiness destroys form and grasp an emptiness that puts an end to things. To put an end to this doubt, they are told 'form is emptiness,' not form is destroyed by emptiness. Third, they wonder if emptiness is a thing and grasp an emptiness that has existence. And to put an end to this doubt, they are told that since 'emptiness is form,' they cannot use emptiness to grasp emptiness. Once these three doubts are put to rest, true emptiness reveals itself.

"If you take form as illusory, it cannot obstruct emptiness. And if you take emptiness as true emptiness, it cannot harm illusory form. If it obstructed form, it would be destructive emptiness, not true emptiness. And if form obstructed emptiness, it would be real form, not illusory form. The *Maha Prajnaparamita Shastra* says, 'If all dharmas were not empty, there would be no path and no attainment.' And according to the *Madhyamaka-karika Shastra*, 'It is because of emptiness that all dharmas come to be.'"

Chen-k'o says, "Ordinary people don't understand. They see form, but they don't see emptiness. Followers of the Two Paths are biased and see emptiness, but they don't see form. It is just like the water of the Ganges. Fishes and dragons see it as a cavernous home. Devas see it as aquamarine. Humans see it as a flowing current. Hungry ghosts see it as a roaring blaze. What these four beings see is nothing but their emotions. Those who wake up understand that none of these exist."

Deva says, "Ordinary people can't conceive of emptiness without eliminating form. Bodhisattvas, regardless of the phenomena, understand that form and emptiness share the same body."

Conze says, "Aristotle pointed out in his *Metaphysics* that the rejection of the principle of contradiction must lead to the conclusion that 'all things are one.' This seemed to him manifestly absurd. Here, conversely, the insight into the oneness of all is the great goal, and only by contradictions can it be attained" (*Buddhist Wisdom Books*, p. 84).

9. The same holds for sensation and perception, memory and consciousness:

evam eva vedana sanjna sanskara vijnanam 受想行識亦復如是

Form is usually listed as the first of the Five Skandhas into which early Buddhists analyzed any given state of awareness. This is because we have become so trapped by our materialistic delusions that our first line of defense in contesting attacks on the validity of our existence is our "body." Certainly this body of ours exists, or so we think. But trying to define our selves in terms of form, we find only emptiness and cannot overcome the indivisibility of "our" form with all forms (the entire external world). Thus, we look elsewhere for a self by considering the remaining four skandhas. Commentators seldom have anything to say about this line of the text, but it is one of the most important lines in the sutra. Without it, a person might limit their understanding of emptiness to its relationship with form. But by extending the same equation to the other four skandhas, Avalokiteshvara treats everything we might think of as our selves in the same light. Thus, all Five Skandhas are emptiness, and emptiness is all Five Skandhas, both individually and as a whole. But how can this be? If emptiness is equal to form, how can it also be equal to the other skandhas? This is because no matter how many skandhas or aspects we analyze our experience into, they are all delusions. They do not exist other than as delusions. Thus, there is no limit to the number of angels that can dance on the head of a pin.

Te-ch'ing says, "If we know that form and emptiness are equal and of one suchness, thought after thought we save others without seeing any others to save, and thought after thought we go in search of buddhahood without seeing any buddhahood to find. Thus we say the perfect mind has no knowledge or attainment. Such a person surpasses bodhisattvas and instantly reaches the other shore of buddhahood. Once you can look upon the skandha of form like this, when you then think about the other four skandhas, they will all be perfectly clear. It's the same as 'when you follow one sense back to its source, all six become free.' Thus it says, 'the same holds for sensation and perception, memory and consciousness.'"

The Buddha told Shariputra, "Form is simply a name. Likewise, sensation, perception, memory, and consciousness are simply names. Shariputra, the self is simply a name. There is no self that can ever be found. And it cannot be found because it is empty" (*Perfection of Wisdom in Twenty-five Thousand Lines*, translated from Sanskrit by Kumarajiva, Chinese Tripitaka, vol. 8, p. 221c).

10. Here, Shariputra, all dharmas are defined by emptiness: *iha shariptura sarva dharmah shunyata lakshana* 舍利子諸法空相

Again, Avalokiteshvara tries to shake Shariputra out of his earlier understanding. Having told the compiler of the earliest texts on the Abhidharma that the Five Skandhas are empty of self-existence, Avalokiteshvara now applies this to all their subsets. The difference is that the skandhas represent a rather simple view of

reality, while the matrix of dharmas, the number of which varied
from sect to sect, represents a more complex attempt to analyze
and explain the world of our experience. A great deal has been
made by some commentators in this shift of analysis from skandhas to dharmas, as if dharmas somehow represented a higher level
of reality. And the same commentators have never tired of viewing the realization of the emptiness of dharmas as representing a
greater insight than the realization of the emptiness of the skandhas. But there is no difference. In fact, the lists of dharmas used
in the matrices of such sects as the Sarvastivadins were arranged
according to which skandha each dharma belonged to. Thus, the
dharmas of the Sarvastivadins covered the same reality extrapolated from the same raw material of awareness as the skandhas.
The only exception was that space and nirvana were included in
their matrices as unconditioned dharmas but excluded from the
skandhas. However, according to the Prajnaparamita, even space
and nirvana are defined by the same emptiness as the skandhas
and thus do not exist outside of the skandhas.

The Sarvastivadins, as their name indicates, believed the doctrine (*vade*) that all (*sarva*) dharmas exist (*asti*) and that the self-
existence (*svabhava*) of dharmas traverses the three periods of
time. The Sarvastivadins were quite familiar with the Buddha's
teaching that the skandhas are empty of a self, but they were not
willing to admit that the skandhas were completely empty. They
believed that each dharma included an underlying substrate, a
defining characteristic that persisted through time. The *Heart
Sutra* counters this by saying that all dharmas are empty of any
self-existent quality, substance, or entity that would set them

apart in time, space, or mind, and that the only sense in which they are real is as emptiness, and that it is only in terms of their emptiness that we can distinguish them at all. Thus, all dharmas are marked, characterized, and distinguished by emptiness and emptiness alone.

It should be noted that the Sarvastivadin conception of dharmas as ultimate, discrete entities was not shared by other sects, such as the Sthaviravadins, who followed up their analysis of experience as a plurality of dharmas with a synthesis showing that such dharmas are not discrete but can only be defined by their relationships with other dharmas. But the *Heart Sutra* was not composed with the Sthaviravadins in mind.

Hui-ching says, "As for 'all dharmas are defined by emptiness,' this means the Five Skandhas, the Twelve Abodes of Sensation, and the Eighteen Elements of Perception are all essentially empty."

Fa-tsang says, "Because dharmas manifest the appearance of emptiness, they are said to be defined by emptiness. To be defined by emptiness means there is no one who grasps and nothing that is grasped. It means without duality."

Deva says, "The *Awakening of Faith in the Mahayana* says, 'What is meant by "dharmas" is the mind. Dharmas don't exist by themselves. Dharmas exist because of the mind.' But then neither does the mind exist by itself. The mind exists because of dharmas. And how so? If there are no dharmas, the mind has nothing to think about. And because it has nothing to think about, there are no dharmas and no mind. Know then that to discriminate is to be deluded. Not to discriminate is to understand the nature of dharmas. This non-discrimination does not mean no discrimination at all. It means the discrimination of discrimination. This is non-discrimination."

11. NOT BIRTH OR DESTRUCTION, PURITY OR DEFILEMENT, COMPLETENESS OR DEFICIENCY:
anutpanna aniruddha amala avimala anuna aparipurnah
不生不滅，不垢不淨，不增不減

This is a restatement of the Buddha's teaching of the Three Insights (*tri-vidya*) into what characterizes a dharma, or fundamental entity of the mind. These are impermanence (*anitya*), suffering (*duhkha*), and no self (*anatman*). This is the basis for the application of the word *dharma* by early Buddhists, and this formula linking impermanence, suffering, and no self is repeated again and again in the canons of the Sarvastivadins and other Buddhist sects. Only those entities marked or defined by these three qualities were of interest to early Buddhists, for only such "things" were seen as having a bearing on their spiritual welfare. This was the origin of the Abhidharma. Thus, houses and trees and sunrises and dogs and governments were not included. The world of dharmas revolved, instead, around such entities as the Five Skandhas, the Twelve Abodes of Sensation, the Eighteen Elements of Perception, the Twelve-Link Chain of Dependent Origination, and the Four Truths.

Here is a typical example of the connection among the Three Insights from what the Sarvastivadins considered the earliest and most authoritative collection of the Buddha's sermons:

Thus have I heard: Once, when the Buddha was dwelling near Shravasti at Anathapindada Garden in Jeta Forest, the Bhagavan told the monks, "Whatever is form is impermanent. And whatever is impermanent is suffering. And whatever is suffering is devoid of a self, devoid of a self and anything that might belong to a self. One who views things like this sees things as they really are. So, too, are sensation, perception, memory and consciousness impermanent. And being impermanent, they are suffering. And being suffering, they are devoid of a self and anything that might belong to a self. One who views things like this sees them as they really are. Those noble disciples who view things like this are repulsed by form and repulsed by sensation, perception, memory, and consciousness. And because they are repulsed by them, they do not delight in them. And because they do not delight in them, they are free of them. And those who are free give rise to the knowledge of how things really are and can claim: 'My life is finally over, I have set forth on the path of purity, I have done what had to be done, and now I know I will experience no future existence.'" Hearing these words of the Buddha, the monks were pleased and put them into practice. (*Samyukt Agama*: 9)

According to the above formula, the fundamental mark (*mula-lakshana*) is impermanence, which itself includes the marks of birth and destruction (the Sarvastivadins inserted duration and aging as well). But if, as Avalokiteshvara tells us, all dharmas are empty of self-existence, impermanence no longer applies, as they neither come into being, nor do they cease to be. The Greek philosopher Heraclitus, a contemporary of the Buddha, declared, "*Hanta pei.*" Everything flows. But if there is no beginning and no end, then there is no impermanence. Impermanence is based on the concept of at least two states of temporal existence: the birth and death of an animate being and the origination and destruction of an inanimate object. In the light of Prajnaparamita, all such states are seen to be empty of self-existence. That is, they do not exist or occur independently of other states and are only divisible on the basis of arbitrary distinctions. The existence of anything in our material or mental universe cannot be determined without positing the existence of something else. Thus, things only exist in relationship with other things. In fact, their very thingness is simply a convenient label for our ignorance of their true nature, which is emptiness. Actually, nothing is born, and nothing is destroyed. The only things that seem to be born or destroyed are the illusions conjured by our misunderstanding. And if we looked closely enough, we would see that these, too, are neither born nor destroyed. According to the Sarvastivadins, in the course of a single day we experience 6,400,099,998 such births and deaths. But each birth and each death is illusory. For birth and death are devoid of anything real. Thus, Avalokiteshvara tells Shariputra that dharmas are neither born nor destroyed.

As the Buddha noted in the short sutra quoted above, it is because of impermanence, it is because something is born and something is destroyed, that there is suffering. The response to this by early Buddhist sects was to embark on a course of practice designed to sever the connection between suffering and impermanence. Suffering only exists because of our attachment to what is impermanent. Thus, attachments are viewed as burdens to be abandoned, as obstructions to be transcended, or here, in the language of the Sarvastivadins, as defilements to be purified. This was the usual view of such things by early Buddhists. The problem with this for later Buddhists, especially those inclined toward the Mahayana, was the practice of repulsion inherent in this teaching. Reflecting on this, many concluded that such a negative attitude was just as likely to result in further attachment as in liberation.

When Hung-jen, the Fifth Patriarch of China's Zen sect, decided it was time to choose an heir, he asked the monks at his temple to express their understanding in a poem. His chief disciple, Shen-hsiu, offered this one: "The body is a bodhi tree / the mind is a spotless mirror / keep it always clean / don't let it gather dust." Hui-neng, whose monastic duties normally kept him busy pounding rice, saw Shen-hsiu's poem and responded with this one: "Bodhi isn't a tree / what's spotless isn't a mirror / actually there isn't a thing / where do you get this dust?" After reading Hui-neng's poem, Hung-jen made him the Sixth Patriarch. And ever since then it has been Hui-neng's understanding, not Shen-hsiu's, that has dominated the teaching of Zen. This is also Avalokiteshvara's point. Since the defining characteristic of all dharmas is their emptiness, they cannot be purified, nor can they be defiled. Thus, the reason the doctrine of suffering no longer applies is that there is nothing that suffers. Or, as Hui-neng might have said, "Where do you get this suffering?"

Of course, impermanence and suffering do arise if there is a self, if there is something subject to impermanence and suffering. But such a self cannot be found. And because such a self cannot be found, dharmas are said to be "empty of self-existence." And being empty of self-existence, dharmas are therefore not complete (*nuna*). But while dharmas lack anything self-existent that would qualify them as "complete," neither are they parts of anything else, for there is nothing that can be distinguished as a part, much less a whole. Therefore, they are not incomplete or deficient (*paripurna*).

The terms *nuna* and *paripurna* have often been interpreted here as meaning "increase" and "decrease." While such translations are possible, they have prevented readers from seeing these three pairs of terms as synonyms for the Three Insights of early Buddhism and have even misled them into seeing these terms as descriptive of emptiness rather than dharmas. Apparently aware of this problem, the authors of the longer version of the *Heart Sutra* replaced *paripurna* with *sanpurna*, which still means "incomplete" or "deficient" but which does not share *paripurna*'s additional meaning of "decrease."

Hui-ching says, "If we see dharmas born, then we see dharmas destroyed. But dharmas are not really born, and they are not destroyed. They are like cataracts that appear as flowers in the sky. They are false appearances that obstruct our eye of wisdom. The attachment to individuality of ordinary people is called defilement, and the realization of the emptiness of the individual is what is meant by purity. But if defilement can be eliminated and can then be called purity, then defilement is essentially empty, and in emptiness there is also no purity. When the reality of suchness is submerged, it doesn't shrink. And when it reappears, it doesn't grow. Bound by attachments, it's called the womb of the tathagatas (*tathagata-garbha*). Unbound, it's called the body of reality (*dharma-kaya*). Although the names vary, its real essence doesn't differ."

Fa-tsang says, "To be neither born nor destroyed is to be an ordinary person at the beginning of the path. To be neither pure nor defiled is to be a bodhisattva at the middle of the path. And to be neither complete nor deficient is to be a buddha at the end of the path. These three have no nature of their own, hence they manifest the marks of true emptiness."

Hui-chung says, "All dharmas are the mind. But the mind has no body or limbs. So how can it be created or destroyed, pure or impure, whole or incomplete?"

Ching-chueh says, "What does not exist earlier but exists now is said to be born. What already exists but then does not exist is said to be destroyed. The assembly of causes and conditions does not result in birth, and the dispersal of causes and conditions does not result in destruction. What is pure or defiled refers to the mind. But the mind is essentially no mind. Thus, what is purified, and what is defiled? It's as if someone dreamt that the pearl of the moon was defiled by falling into muddy water, and they tried to wash it clean and then awoke and realized that the moon was not in the water and had never been defiled and that washing it hadn't purified it, that it had always been pure."

Pao-t'ung says, "Let the Four Elements and Five Skandhas be born and die in vain. They have no effect on our dharma body.

Like bamboo shadows on the steps, they can't be swept away. Like the moon moving across the water, it doesn't leave a trace. Our dharma body is pure. It has no blemish, stain or smudge. It can't be damaged or burned. Like a lotus, it doesn't touch the water. Nor does this body whose heart is pure and empty become greater for a sage or lesser for a fool. It is simply so and changeless."

Part Two

Abhidharma in the Light of Prajnaparamita

12/13. THEREFORE, SHARIPUTRA, IN EMPTINESS
THERE IS NO FORM, / NO SENSATION, NO PERCEPTION,
NO MEMORY AND NO CONSCIOUSNESS:
*tasmac shariputra shunyatayan na rupan na vedana na
sanjna na sanskarah na vijnanam*
是故(舍利子)空中無色, 無受想行識

HAVING INTRODUCED Shariputra to the Prajnaparamita, Avalokiteshvara now reviews the
major categories of the Sarvastivadin Abhi-
dharma in its light, which is the light of emptiness. Thus, the
focus here is "in emptiness" (*shunyatayan*), where *shunyata* is in
the locative case. In the light of convention, objects are real. In
the light of meditation, objects are not real, but dharmas are. In
the light of wisdom, objects and dharmas are not real, nor are
they not real. They are not real, because they are empty of self-
existence. But neither are they not real, because they are empty
of non-existence. Emptiness is what makes everything real. Self-
existence and non-existence are what make everything false.

When we establish a dharma that either exists or does not
exist, we create a separation in time, in space, and in our minds.

Emptiness is not space but the absence of space. Dharmas represent the creation of space, the conjuring of division into our awareness. Emptiness represents the removal of that space or division. Thus, where there is emptiness, which is everywhere, there are no dharmas. Dharmas as self-existent or non-existent entities are fictions. Dharmas as emptiness are real. Thus, the separation of dharmas from emptiness is impossible. Dharmas cannot be separated from emptiness. They are not outside emptiness, and they are not inside emptiness. They are emptiness. The same holds for emptiness. It is not outside dharmas and not inside them. Neither dharmas nor emptiness can fit inside the other. They are co-extensive. This is true of form and also true of sensation, perception, memory, and consciousness. They do not exist in emptiness; they are one with emptiness. And emptiness is one with them, with each of them, and with all of them. Emptiness is not just their common denominator, it is their only denominator. Dharmas are defined by emptiness alone, not by permanence or impermanence, not by purity or impurity, not by the presence or the absence of a self. Emptiness is their real nature.

Conze says, "Everything that is at all worth knowing is contained in the Hridaya. But it can be found there only if spiritual insight is married to intellectual ability, and coupled with a delight in the use of the intellect. This Sutra, it is true, points to something that lies far beyond the intellect. But the way to get to that is to follow the intellect as far as it will take you. And the dialectical logic of this Sutra enables the intellect, working through language, to carry the understanding a stage further than the conceptual thinking based on ordinary logic can do" (*Buddhist Wisdom Books*, p. 99).

Hui-chung says, "The nature of dharmas is fundamentally empty, thus it says 'in emptiness.' Form cannot be found, thus it says 'no form.' Likewise, the mind cannot be found, thus it says, 'no sensation, no perception, no memory, and no consciousness.'"

Te-ch'ing says, "The reason the true emptiness of prajna is forever free of any defect is because it is pure and contains nothing. Thus, there is no trace of the Five Skandhas."

Chen-k'o says, "Once ice melts into water, it becomes square in a square container and round in a round container. The square and round containers represent the world before us. Although the world before us is born and destroyed, pure and defiled, complete and deficient, it is like water that has become ice, it is completely hard. For practitioners who know this, the Twelve Abodes of Sensation, the Eighteen Elements of Perception, the Twelve Links, and the Four Truths are all clear. Still, the world cannot empty itself, it requires reflection to empty the world."

Ching-mai says, "When the sutra says that we do not see the appearance of birth of the skandha of form, nor the appearance of its destruction, the appearance of its purity or the appearance of its defilement, and that the other skandhas up to consciousness are the same, it is because their natures are empty. In emptiness how could there be birth or destruction, oneness or division?

"If form really existed, it would be different from emptiness. The Five Skandhas would then exist in emptiness. But bodhisattvas use their true knowledge of reality to see that the skandha of form to which people cling is essentially empty and non-existent. It is because of the existence of form and the other skandhas that suffering also exists. But if form and the other skandhas are empty, then we are rescued from suffering.

"The *Madhyamaka Shastra* says, 'An effect arises from multiple causes, but these causes do not exist by themselves. But if causes have no self-existence, then they do not really exist. And if causes themselves do not exist, how can they give rise to an effect?' Thus, the purity or defilement of form and the other skandhas does not arise from causes, nor does it not arise from causes."

14. NO EYE, NO EAR, NO NOSE, NO TONGUE, NO BODY AND NO MIND: *na cakshuh shrotra ghrana jihva kaya manansi* 無眼耳鼻舌身意

In analyzing the possible constituents of our world of awareness, early Buddhists did not limit themselves to the Five Skandhas but used several other conceptual frameworks. After the skandhas, the next most common analytical scheme involved a division of our awareness into the Twelve Abodes, or *ayatanas*. The word *ayatana* means "resting place" and refers to the location in a home where a family kept its sacred fire. Thus, its use by Buddhists was meant to appeal to Brahmans and at the same time to redirect their spiritual endeavors to the sanctuary within us all. But instead of focusing on one ayatana, the Buddha directed his disciples to examine twelve locations, any one of which could be considered the abode of the sacred fire of our awareness.

As with the Five Skandhas, the Twelve Abodes also break

down our experience into a series of components. But while the Five Skandhas summarize what we think of as the external world into one component and what we think of as the internal world into four components, the ayatanas divide the external skandha of form among ten of its twelve abodes and the remaining four skandhas of sensation, perception, memories, and consciousness between only two abodes. Obviously, such a scheme betrays a strong materialist origin that probably predated the Buddha and that he simply took over due to its general acceptance.

This scheme usually begins, as it does here, with the six abodes of our sensory powers, or *indriya*: eyes (*cakshu*), ears (*shrotra*), nose (*ghrana*), tongue (*jihva*), body (*kaya*), and mind (*manana*). They are called *indriya*, or powers, because they are sufficiently miraculous to make us wonder if they were not conferred on us by the Vedic god Indra, the all-powerful King of Heaven. According to the Sarvastivadins, the first five of these powers can also be divided into two components: a primary component similar to what we would call a nerve and a secondary component consisting of that nerve's organ of sensation. Unlike the first five, the sixth power, the mind, was not conceived as having any such physical or neurological basis. It was not based on the brain or the spinal cord but was purely experiential. And it was not only the source of the raw material for this scheme, it was the source of the scheme itself.

But, as with the skandhas, in a world where nothing exists by itself, where every division of one thing from another is a mis-perception—or misconception—of the way things really are, there are no eyes, ears, nose, tongue, body, or mind. We cannot, for example, draw a line around the eyes that is not necessarily arbitrary. There is no point at which the eyes begin or end, either in time or in space or conceptually. The eye bone is connected to the face bone, and the face bone is connected to the head bone, and the head bone is connected to the neck bone, and so it goes down to the toe bone, the floor bone, the earth bone, the worm bone, the dreaming butterfly bone. Thus, what we call our eyes are so many bubbles in a sea of foam. This is not only true of our eyes but of our other powers of sensation as well, including the mind.

When Hui-k'o asked Bodhidharma to help him make his mind stop, the First Patriarch of Zen said, "Show me this mind of yours, and I'll make it stop." Hui-k'o answered, "But I've looked everywhere, and I can't find the mind." Bodhidharma said, "There. I've stopped it for you." Thus, in the light of emptiness, we say that the eyes and the other powers do not exist, which does not mean that we have no eyes, only that the eyes are not ultimately real, just a convenient fiction to which we give a name. In the comments that follow, readers should note that the Chinese prefer to call the Six Powers the "Six Roots," or "Six Bases" of sensation.

Hui-chung says, "This refers to the 'Six Roots.' People steadfastly cling to delusion as real. This is why the various kinds of bad karma arise. This is why they're called 'roots.' As long as each root gathers karma and nourishes life, the countless obstructions of mistaken identity never end. These Six Roots of our knowledge are centered on the mind. If the mind can be stilled, the roots and their domains will be empty and suddenly clear.

Thus it says, 'no eyes, no ears, no nose, no tongue, no body and no mind.'"

Hui-ching says, "The tissue of the eye is the element of earth, its tears are the element of water, its warmth is the element of fire, and its movements are the element of wind. But is the element of earth the eye? No. Or are the elements of water, fire, or wind the eye? The Four Elements are not the eye. Each of the Four Elements has its differences, which we call its individual characteristics. When we combine them to form the eye, we call this its joint characteristics. In the absence of the Four Elements, there is no self-existent eye. When the Four Elements are present, the eye has no other nature. And having no individual nature and no other nature, the eye is then empty. But although the nature of the eye is empty, it is not the case that there is no eye. This is also true of the other senses."

15. NO SHAPE, NO SOUND, NO SMELL, NO TASTE, NO FEELING AND NO THOUGHT: *na rupa shabda gandha rasa sprashtavya dharmah* 無色聲香味觸法

In addition to six powers of sensation, the Twelve Abodes include six domains, or *vishaya*. The word *vishaya* means "territory" or "dimension" and refers to the domains in which our powers of sensation function. These domains are shape (*rupa*), sound (*shabda*), smell (*gandha*), taste (*rasa*), feeling (*sparsha*), and thought (*dharma*). The reason these were called domains rather than objects is that an object presumes the further application of perceptual categories. Thus, there are not necessarily any objects, only domains. And each of these domains is separate from the others. The eye, for example, has no access to the domain of sound, and the ear has no access to the domain of shape. While this is obviously true for five of our powers, the Sarvastivadins argued that the mind is an exception, that it can hear and see, that not only can it think thoughts, it can also experience what arises when any of our powers comes into contact with its corresponding domain. Thus, it is able to fabricate a set of categories to use in the other domains of sensation.

Together, these Six Powers and Six Domains comprise the Twelve Abodes by means of which we can trace and locate whatever we know of our experience. But like the skandhas, these ayatanas also turn out to be devoid of a self, or anything that might be called self-existent. Of course, someone might say we would not normally look for our self in the abode of the ear or in the abode of sound. Normally, we would look for our self in the abode of the mind or in the abode of thought. Surely this is where we can find our self. But what we find in our mind and our thought is the same as what we find in our ear and in sound: an ocean in constant flux. Just as our ear turns out to be nothing but a construct, and likewise sound, neither can we isolate anything we might call our mind or thought, much less our self. This is what an examination of the Twelve Abodes teaches us. They all turn out to be arbitrary distinctions cut from the seamless fabric of reality, or as Avalokiteshvara might say, from the seamless fabric of emptiness. Thus, Avalokiteshvara's point is to push practitioners, such as the Sarvastivadins, one more step, beyond the Twelve Abodes to which they had become attached.

Satisfied that there is no self among the Twelve Abodes, the Sarvastivadins stopped their self-analysis and assumed that the Twelve Abodes themselves were real. But the only sense in which they are real is in their emptiness. Thus, there are no eyes or ears or mind and no shape or sound or thought.

Hui-ching says, "If the Six Roots [powers] exist, then the Six Kinds of Dust [domains] cannot be empty. But having determined that the eye is empty, its dust clearly does not exist. Why are they called 'roots'? Because they can give rise to the various kinds of consciousness. And why are they called 'dust'? Because they defile the pure mind."

16. NO ELEMENT OF PERCEPTION, FROM EYE TO CONCEPTUAL CONSCIOUSNESS: *na cakshur-dhatur yavan na manovijnanan-dhatuh* 無眼界乃至無意識界

Although this line seems like a continuation of the previous two lines, it actually represents a different scheme of analysis. I've amended it slightly and added the word "perception" to make the meaning clearer and the language less awkward. A literal rendering of the Sanskrit would be "no element of eye up to no element of conceptual consciousness."

The elements (*dhatu*) to which this line refers present a more balanced and dynamic scheme than that of the Twelve Abodes, as they add the Six Kinds of Consciousness (*vijnana*) that arise when the Six Powers and Six Domains of Sensation come into contact. These include visual, auditory, olfactory, gustatory, and tactile consciousness, as well as conceptual consciousness.

Together, these Eighteen Elements provide a more detailed explanation of any particular state of awareness, presenting it as a combination of one or more triads. Here, as was also common in such sutra collections as the *Samyukt Agama*, Avalokiteshvara condenses these eighteen and cites only the first of the Six Powers and the last of the Six Kinds of Consciousness. But all eighteen are meant.

While the first twelve of these elements are no different from those dealt with earlier, the additional six provide a closer look at consciousness, especially conceptual consciousness (*manovijnana*). According to the Sarvastivadins, this consciousness functions not only in the domain of thought but also in the other five domains, where it gives rise to the categories by means of which the other kinds of consciousness discriminate shape, sound, smell, taste, and feeling, and where it, in turn, arises as it comes into contact with these five forms of consciousness that then become its *de facto* organ of perception. Thus, according to this circular scheme, conceptual consciousness includes our consciousness of thoughts and concepts but also our consciousness of perception in general.

In reviewing this three-part scheme, a number of commentators have described the Six Kinds of Consciousness as representing the subjective elements of our experience, the Six Powers as the objective elements, and the Six Domains as the conditioning elements. The problem with such a distinction is that it easily becomes counterproductive. This three-part scheme of powers, domains, and consciousness was developed to allow practitioners the opportunity to investigate the nature of their experience and ascertain for themselves the absence or presence of a self. To call certain elements "subjective" reintroduces the self in sheep's clothing. The best approach is to give each element equal weight. The same problem arises from distinguishing certain skandhas or ayatanas as internal or external. These are judgments, which can be useful up to a point, but which easily mislead us into sneaking a "self" through the back door, and which should not be considered as anything more than convenient labels.

Although all eighteen of these elements are not necessarily present at any one moment, and certain beings might lack one or more sets of elements, this scheme still provided as detailed an explanation of our perceptual experience as anyone might want, or need. In meditating upon these elements, we can see that they are equally impermanent, equally subject to suffering, and equally lacking a self or anything that might belong to a self. However, Avalokiteshvara goes further and denies that any of these categories have any validity to begin with. Such is the light of Prajnaparamita.

Hui-chung says, "This refers to the Eighteen Elements. The sutra abbreviates and cites the eye element, but all the elements are meant. Because the Six Roots give rise to the Six Kinds of Dust, and the Six Kinds of Dust give rise to the Six Kinds of Consciousness, they are known as the Eighteen Elements, an element being what produces the different kinds of discrimination."

Pao-t'ung says, "Because we have eyes, we sense forms. Because we have forms, we sense perceptions. Because we have perceptions, we sense memories. Because we have memories, we sense consciousness. Because we have consciousness, we have the names and appearances of the Six Senses. Following such sights and sounds, we wander through life and death without cease. To put an end to life and death, if you can just see through one sense, you will immediately be at peace and resume being the person you were before the last empty kalpa began."

Chen-k'o says, "The Five Skandhas are the Twelve Abodes of Sensation, and the Twelve Abodes of Sensation are the Eighteen Elements of Perception. The Buddha realized everyone's capacities are different and adapted his teachings accordingly. For those deluded about the mind but not form, he taught the Five Skandhas. For those deluded about form but not the mind, he taught the Twelve Abodes of Sensation. And for those deluded about both mind and form, he taught the Eighteen Elements of Perception. Essentially, the skandhas, the abodes, and the elements do not go beyond form and mind."

Hui-ching says, "If our self is in the eyes, then it cannot be in the ears. And if there is a self present in each element, then a person would be a combination of eighteen selves. And if none of the elements has a self, then there would not be a self in their combination. And because there is none, we know the self is not a real entity.

"Someone might ask, 'The eye depends on the dust [domain] of shape, and the ear depends on the dust of sound, and so on, and the mind depends on the dust of thought. The first five roots and five kinds of dust can all be perceived. What about the dust of thought on which the mind depends? What is it like? The five senses [powers] are paired with the five kinds of dust of sensation and together give rise to five kinds of consciousness. Although the five roots can see and hear and feel, they cannot discriminate. They have to rely on the simultaneous discrimination of the conceptual consciousness. It is just such distinctions that make up the dust of thought.'"

Chih-shen says, "If the Six Roots exist, then the Six Kinds of Dust on which they depend must be real. But if we find that the Six Roots are empty, then the Six Kinds of Dust on which they depend cannot be real. Thus it says 'no shape, no sound, no smell, no taste, no feeling and no thought.' For Hinayana followers, when causes come together, dharmas arise, and when causes separate, dharmas cease. Followers of the Mahayana look at this differently. When causes come together, dharmas do not arise, and when causes separate, dharmas do not cease. Thus, it says, 'no element of perception, from eye to conceptual consciousness.'"

17. NO CAUSAL LINK, FROM IGNORANCE TO OLD AGE AND DEATH: *na avidya na avidya kshayo* 無無明亦無無明盡

Having analyzed our experience in terms of skandhas, abodes, and elements, we now consider it as a sequence of causal connections. Of course, in the light of prajna, these causal connections dissolve, as do the skandhas, the abodes, and the elements. Still, this sequence, known as the Twelve Links (*dvadashanga*) of Dependent Origination (*pratitya-samutpada*), remains one of the most powerful teachings of the Buddha and is worth studying in detail.

In Sanskrit, this line reads "no ignorance and no end of ignorance," and the next line reads "up to no old age and death and no end of old age and death." To avoid the awkwardness of the second line, I have amended both lines and at the same time returned to the traditional presentation of this sequence as it occurs in the sutras of the *Samyukt Agama* and elsewhere, where the Buddha deals first with the links in the Chain of Dependent Origination and then with putting an end to them. Here, only ignorance (*avidya*) and old age and death (*jara-marana*) are mentioned and the intervening links omitted for the sake of brevity. To clarify the subject matter, I have also added the phrase "causal link," which does not occur in the Sanskrit.

As to the origin of this formula, in the *Samyukt Agama* the Buddha says that this is simply the Dharma and neither his creation nor the creation of anyone else. On the night of his Enlightenment, Shakyamuni asked himself what is the source of suffering and answered that it is old age and death. He then asked what is the origin of old age and death and answered that it is birth (*jati*), and the origin of birth is existence (*bhava*), and the origin of existence is attachment (*upadana*), and the origin of attachment is thirst (*trishna*), and the origin of thirst is sensation (*vedana*), and the origin of sensation is contact (*sparsha*), and the origin of contact is the abodes (*ayatana*), and the origin of the abodes is name and form (*nama-rupa*), and the origin of name and form is consciousness (*vijnana*), and the origin of consciousness is memory (*sanskara*), and the origin of memory is ignorance.

According to the Buddha, ignorance means to mistake the true for the false and the false for the true. Thus, ignorance includes not only the absence of knowledge but also the presence of delusion. In his standard explanation of these terms in the *Samyukt Agama,* the Buddha said ignorance consists in being ignorant of cause and effect and ignorant of the way things are; memory consists in our habitual patterns of speech, action, and thought; consciousness consists in the six forms of sensory consciousness; name consists in the four formless skandhas and form in the skandha of form; the abodes consist in the six senses; contact consists in the six kinds of sensory contact; sensation consists in what is pleasurable, painful, and neutral; thirst consists in thirst for the Realm of Desire, thirst for the Realm of Form, and thirst for the Formless Realm; attachment consists in attachment to desires, attachment to views, attachment to rules, and attachment to a self; existence consists in existence in the Realm of Desire, existence in the Realm of Form, and existence in the Formless Realm; birth consists in obtaining a body; and old age and death consist in losing a body (cf. *Samyukt Agama:* 298).

Later Buddhist commentators, such as Buddhaghosha, interpreted the first two links of ignorance and memory as representing causes from a past existence, the last two links of birth and old age and death as representing effects for a future existence, and the intervening eight links as representing effects experienced in the present (consciousness through sensation) or causes produced in the present (desire, attachment, and existence). While such a formulation is useful in clarifying the relationship among these links, in the hands of some commentators it has reintroduced the concept of a "soul" through the back door of rebirth. Hence, readers will want to consider such a conception in the light of its usefulness in their own practice before employing it.

The essential point is to realize that this sequence goes round and round, forward and backward, and accounts for any particular experience we might focus on without recourse to a self. Thus, it plants the seed of our liberation. We know that whatever link we might identify with at any moment has been produced by the previous link and will in turn give rise to the succeeding link without help from a self of any kind. If we can break but one link in this chain, it comes to an end. But if the links of this chain do not include a self, then it is already broken. Thus, how can there be suffering, if there is no one who suffers? By meditating upon this, we can liberate ourselves from our selves and put an end to this chain of causation once and for all, which is what the Buddha did. This is also what Avalokiteshvara now does, as he shines the light of Prajnaparamita on these links and finds that they do not exist in the first place. Thus, there is no need to put an end to what does not exist.

Hui-chung says, "Deluded people cling to the existence of the Five Skandhas and the Eighteen Elements and obstruct their own nature and don't see its light. This is what is meant by 'ignorance.' Once they discover the nature of their own mind, the roots and dust of sensation turn out to be empty at heart, and conceptual consciousness ceases to function. How could there be any obstruction? Therefore it says 'no ignorance.'"

Buddhadasa says, "Being here now is Dependent Origination of the middle way of ultimate truth. . . . In the Suttas, it is said that the highest right view, the supramundane right view, is the view that is neither eternalism nor annihilationism, which can be had by the power of understanding Dependent Origination. Dependent Origination is in the middle between the ideas of having a self and the total lack of self. It has its own principle: 'Because there is this, there is that; because this is not, that is not'" (*Paticcasamuppada: Practical Dependent Origination*, pp. 7-9).

18. AND NO END OF CAUSAL LINK, FROM IGNORANCE TO OLD AGE AND DEATH: *yavan na jaramaranan na jaramarana kshayo* 乃至無老死亦無老死盡

Having told Shariputra that in the light of Prajnaparamita the links of this chain do not exist, Avalokiteshvara now tells him that in the same light, their non-existence also does not exist. There cannot be an end of causation, if there is no causation in the first place.

As with the previous line, I have amended my translation to agree with the traditional presentation of the Chain of Dependent Origination, which goes as follows: After reflecting on the truth of Dependent Origination, Shakyamuni realized that suffering would cease if old age and death would cease, and old age and death would cease if birth would cease, and birth would cease if existence would cease, and existence would cease if attachment would cease, and attachment would cease if thirst would cease, and thirst would cease if sensation would cease, and sensation would cease if contact would cease, and contact would cease if the abodes would cease, and the abodes would cease if name and form would cease, and name and form would cease if consciousness would cease, and consciousness would cease if memory would cease, and memory would cease if ignorance would cease. And realizing that in this chain of endless transient events there is no self, Shakyamuni broke its links forever and realized Enlightenment.

In one of the sutras that make up the *Samyukt Agama*, Rahula asks his father for instruction. Knowing his son was not yet ready for the highest teaching, Shakyamuni taught him to meditate on the Five Skandhas. Afterward, Rahula returned and asked again for instruction. Knowing he was still not ready, the Buddha taught him to meditate on the Elements of Perception. Afterward, Rahula returned and asked again. Knowing he was still not ready, the Buddha taught him to meditate on the Chain of Dependent Origination. But this time he told him also to meditate on the meaning of the skandhas, the elements, and dependent origination. Retiring to a quiet place, Rahula did as he was instructed and realized that they all led to nirvana. When he returned and reported this to his father, the Buddha knew he was ready and taught him the doctrine of universal impermanence: The eyes, shape, visual consciousness, and visual contact are all impermanent. Retiring to meditate on this, Rahula realized the nature of all dharmas and attained the liberation of an arhan (*Samyukt Agama*: 200)

Hui-chung says, "If the dust and domains of sensation exist, they can end. But because they don't really exist, what is there that ends? 'End' means 'death.' If the twelve links of causation arise, then life and death can end. But because causation does not arise, there is no end of life and death."

Fa-tsang says, "Because its nature is empty, we say there is no ignorance. But because of true emptiness, there is nothing that can end."

Deva says, "The deluded mind grasps appearances and clings to them without let up. This is called 'ignorance.' To understand its source is to bring it to an end. Although there is the end and the not yet ended and the change of appearance from grasping to letting go, in the ultimate body of reality there is no change. Thus it says 'there is no ignorance nor is there an end of ignorance.'"

Ming-k'uang says, "According to the principles of the Four Teachings, there are four kinds of Dependent Origination. Dependent Origination involving birth and death is the Hinayana Teaching for shravakas of inferior capacity. Dependent Origination involving no birth or death is the Common Teaching for pratyeka buddhas of medium capacity. Dependent Origination involving the infinite is the Special Teaching for bodhisattvas of superior capacity. And Dependent Origination involving the unconditioned is the Complete Teaching for bodhisattvas of the highest capacity."

Hui-ching says, "Because bodhisattvas possess great wisdom in which the mind and the world both vanish, they do not share the common view of truth and thus harbor no ignorance. And because they possess great compassion by means of which they teach other beings, they do not enter nirvana and thus do not put an end to ignorance."

19. NO SUFFERING, NO SOURCE, NO RELIEF, NO PATH:
na duhkha samudaya nirodha marga 無苦集滅道

As he nears the end of the Sarvastivadin Abhidharma, Avaloki-teshvara comes to the Four Truths. Just as the previous line sum-marizes the basis of the Buddha's Enlightenment, this line repeats the subject of his first sermon. His audience on that occa-sion included the five ascetics: Ashvajit, Vashpa, Mahanaman, Bhadrika, and Kaundinya. All of these men were related to Shakyamuni. Kaundinya, for example, was his maternal uncle, and Ashvajit was his cousin. All five had been ordered by King Suddhodana to accompany his headstrong son on his spiritual quest. But six years later, when Shakyamuni decided not to con-tinue his austerities but to seek a middle path between austerity and indulgence, they left him in disgust at the shore of the Nairanjana River below the caves they had shared at Pragbodhi. While the five ascetics proceeded to Varanasi, Shakyamuni waded across the river to Bodh Gaya, sat down beneath an ash-vattha tree (*Ficus religiosa*, the Indian fig), and resolved not to rise again until he could put an end to suffering, which he did over the next several days to the benefit of all beings. Not long after his Enlightenment, the Buddha caught up with his former companions just outside Varanasi at a place called Deer Park and proclaimed to them the Four Truths.

As with the previous analytical categories, the Four Truths address the same basic issue: the nature of our experience. The Five Skandhas explained it in terms of aspects or bodies, the Twelve Abodes explained it in terms of locations, the Eighteen

Elements of Perception explained it in terms of components, and the Twelve Links of Dependent Origination explained it in terms of causal connections. It was this last insight that formed the basis of the Buddha's Enlightenment. Hence, it was only natural that he made this the subject of his first sermon. But instead of explaining the entire sequence of Dependent Origination, the Buddha taught his former colleagues a briefer version, and one that included a course of practice as well.

The Buddha began at the same point where he began when he discovered the Chain of Dependent Origination; he began with suffering. But instead of tracing suffering through a chain of causal connections, from old age and death back to ignorance, he focused on one cause in particular, that of thirst (*trishna*), thirst for the existence or non-existence of some object or state to which we become attached. Because all objects and states are subject to change, our thirst and its consequent attachment result in suffering. Thus, the Buddha's First Truth was the truth of suffering (*duhkha*), and the Second Truth was the origination (*samudaya*) of suffering. After announcing these two truths, the Buddha then proclaimed the Third Truth, which was the cessation (*nirodha*) of suffering. If thirst results in attachment and attachment results in suffering, then putting an end to thirst and attachment must result in an end of suffering. The Fourth Truth was the path (*marga*) that led to the end of suffering.

In ancient India, doctors used the same formulation in their profession: the determination of disease, the determination of its source, the determination of relief, and the application of a remedy. While this is roughly the same as Shakyamuni's Four

Truths, the Buddha applied this perspective to a much broader range of experience, to dis-ease, and not simply disease. Thus, Shakyamuni was called the Great Physician.

Many Buddhist masters have said that the Buddha's teaching consists in nothing more than this: suffering and the cessation of suffering. The Buddha often said as much himself. In the *Testament Sutra*, the Buddha says, "The moon can turn hot, and the sun can turn cold, but the Four Truths are not subject to change."

Whether we consider our experience in psychological or physical terms, whether as *nama* or as *rupa*, whether as skandhas, abodes of sensation, elements of perception, or a chain of causation, every experience of which we are aware is transient and fraught with suffering. And every experience is fraught with suffering because we do not see things as they really are, as no things. All we see are what we love and hate and have deceived ourselves into believing exists or does not exist. In response to this, the Buddha asks us to see things as they really are. He does not ask us to cling to optimistic views of eternity or pessimistic views of annihilation but simply to examine our experience. This is the First Truth. It should be noted that "truth" here is a translation of *satya*, which also means "reality." This is the first statement concerning the way things are. Because we are attached to what is impermanent, every experience is doomed to result in suffering. Since attachments are the result of desire, which is the Second Truth, if we can put an end to desire, we can put an end to attachments and thus suffering. This is the Third Truth. Buddhist cultivation, therefore, focuses on our desire for things that do not exist, but which we think exist. The cultivation that leads to seeing things as they really are and thus puts an end to suffering is summarized by the Fourth Truth, which is usually defined as the Eightfold Path: Right Views, Right Intention, Right Speech, Right Action, Right Livelihood, Right Effort, Right Mindfulness, and Right Concentration. As we cultivate this path and turn our thoughts, words, and deeds from what is wrong (*mithya*) to what is right (*samyak*), this becomes the Eightfold Noble (*arya*) Path, and the Four Truths become the Four Noble Truths. By "right" is meant the Middle Way between extremes.

The *Heart Sutra* has been interpreted by some as a summary of the Four Truths as understood in the light of Prajnaparamita. Of course, any Buddhist text can be understood in one way or another as being about the Four Truths. But this interpretation goes further and claims that the *Heart Sutra* is structured around the Four Truths. Support for this interpretation can be found in Edward Conze's "The Prajna-paramita-hridaya Sutra" in *Thirty Years of Buddhist Studies* (pp. 157–165), where he cites relevant portions of the *Perfection of Wisdom in Twenty-five Thousand Lines* and the *Perfection of Wisdom in One Hundred Thousand Lines*. This interpretation goes back to Haribhadra (c. 800) and before him to Maitreya (c. 350). But it is both artificial and unnecessary. Just because we can put a bird in a cage does not mean it belongs in a cage.

The Buddha's sermon on the Four Truths has been called the First Turning of the Wheel, and the teaching of Prajnaparamita has been called the Second Turning of the Wheel. In the traditional formula of the First Truth, suffering is equated with the

Five Skandhas, with which it is necessarily co-extensive. But since the Five Skandhas are empty of self-existence, suffering must also be empty of self-existence. But if suffering is empty of self-existence, then there is no self that suffers. Thus, in emptiness there is no suffering, no source of suffering, no relief from suffering, and no path leading to relief from suffering. This is the basis of Avalokiteshvara's interpretation of the Four Truths.

Hui-ching says, "After the Bhagavan attained Enlightenment, he turned the twelve-spoked Wheel of the Dharma [so-called because of the twelve links in the Chain of Dependent Origination] three times for the five mendicants at Deer Park. With the first turn he explained appearances: 'Monks, this is suffering, this is its source, this is its relief, and this is the path.' With the second turn he explained cultivation: 'Monks, this is suffering, which you should know. This is its source, which you should cut off. This is its relief, which you should realize. And this is the path, which you should practice.' And with the third turn he explained realization: 'Monks, this is suffering, which I now know. This is its source, which I have cut off. This is its relief, which I have realized. And this is the path, which I have practiced.' The Buddha taught the Four Truths to give his followers a place to rest. Now we hear that there is no suffering, source, relief, or path. Suffering does not arise, so how can it exist? Its source produces nothing, so how can it be cut off? Its relief relieves nothing, so what is there to realize? And the path has no form, so how can it be practiced? If there is someone who can practice, then there must be a path to practice. But there is no person and no path, for both individuals and dharmas are empty. To see this is to realize the truth of suchness. Once you shine the light of prajna, individuals and dharmas are both empty. But if the person does not exist, where can there be suffering? Thus, the first truth is not real, and the same is true of the other three."

Ching-chueh says, "Suffering and its source are fundamentally empty. Like tortoise fur, they do not exist. Relief and the path aren't real. Like rabbit horns, they, too, do not exist. These Four Truths are basically empty. In emptiness there are no truths. This emptiness undoes the deluded views of shravakas concerning the truths of origination and annihilation."

Deva says, "For those sunk in worldly desires, there exists the agony of the source of suffering. For those aloof from the world, there exists the path of relief from suffering. Bodhisattvas are between these two. They don't see any source of suffering to relinquish. And they don't see any path of relief to seek. Their thoughts of grasping and letting go cease, and they forget about suffering and happiness."

Hui-chung says, "This elucidates the Four Truths. When the mind seeks something, it becomes attached, and this is the 'truth.' Diligently cultivating realization without pause is the truth of suffering. Poring over scriptures in search of subtle doctrines is the truth of the source. Putting an end to delusions and trying to reach nirvana is the truth of relief. Transcending passion and confusion and pondering the doctrines of the Buddha is the truth of the path. But now, let us consider the Four Noble Truths as medicine for the foregoing illnesses. The mind is already pure and numinous and doesn't require cultivation or realization. This is the truth of suffering. Our nature contains all dharmas. What is there to seek? This is the truth of the source. Delusions don't arise, because we are already in nirvana. This is the truth of relief. Nirvana is neither this nor that, and there is no mistaking right and wrong. This is the truth of the path. This is the physician's explanation. If you understand there is no mind, how can there be Four Truths? Therefore it says, 'no suffering, no source, no relief, no path.'"

Te-ch'ing says, "Not only are there no skandhas, there are no powers of sensation. Not only are there no powers of sensation, there are no domains of sensation. Not only are there no domains of sensation, there are no varieties of consciousness. These powers and domains of sensation and varieties of consciousness, these are the dharmas of ordinary people. The true emptiness of prajna is free of these. Thus it says, 'no' to all of them. But not only do the dharmas of ordinary people not exist in emptiness, neither do the dharmas of sages. The Four Truths are the dharmas of shravakas. The Twelve Links of the Chain of Dependent Origination are the dharmas of pratyekas, with their operation comprising the truths of suffering and the source of suffering and their cessation comprising the truths of relief and the path. But the essence of prajna contains none of these. Not only do the dharmas of shravakas and pratyekas not exist, neither do the dharmas of bodhisattvas."

20. NO KNOWLEDGE, NO ATTAINMENT
AND NO NON-ATTAINMENT: *na jnanan na praptir na-apraptih*
無智無得(亦無無得)

If, as Avalokiteshvara tells Shariputra, dharmas are not fraught with suffering, then the origin of suffering does not exist, and the cessation of suffering is not possible, and there is no path leading to the cessation of suffering. If this is true, it would have left the Sarvastivadins without any truths worth knowing. But for the Sarvastivadins, the acquisition of knowledge was the *sine qua non* of spiritual practice. In my introduction, I mentioned that one of their earliest and most important texts was Katyaya-niputra's *Abhidharma Jnanaprasthana* (The Source of Knowledge through the Study of Dharmas). The Sarvastivadins constructed their entire edifice of practice around a knowledge of the Four Truths and considered them the highest expression of truth. However, they also realized that the traditional formulation of the Four Truths, whereby desire was seen as the origin of suffering, was only valid in the Realm of Desire and that knowledge based on these truths was not complete.

In passing beyond the Realm of Desire and advancing through the Realms of Form and Formlessness, they realized a different kind of knowledge was needed. Although beings in these higher realms were still subject to suffering, their suffering was not caused by desire. Thus, a second formulation of the Four Truths was made whereby the origin of suffering was said to be delusion or ignorance rather than desire. Thus, the Sarvasti-vadins sought eight kinds of knowledge: the Four Truths as they apply to the Realm of Desire and the Four Truths as they apply to the Realms of Form and Formlessness.

In addition, the Sarvastivadins added a ninth and a tenth kind of knowledge for those who successfully cultivated the first eight. These included the knowledge of no more views and the knowledge of no further rebirth. These last two kinds of knowledge were synonymous with nirvana and represented the final goal of the arhan, the hero of the shravaka path. But all ten kinds of knowledge dissolve in the light of the Prajnaparamita, for if there is no suffering, there can be no liberation from suffering. Thus, there is no knowledge of the Four Truths. And if there is no knowledge, there cannot be any attainment (*prapti*) or non-attainment (*aprapti*).

According to the Sarvastivadins, however we might characterize our experience, at any given moment it includes one of these two dharmas of attainment or non-attainment. Sometimes we try to possess something, and sometimes we try not to possess something. For example, when we express our greed, the dharma of attainment is present. And when we express our renunciation of greed, the dharma of non-attainment is present. But even though non-attainment is conducive to higher states of realization, it is still seen as a dharma that also needs to be "non-attained." The Sarvastivadin explanation of how this comes about is not at all clear and seems a little like trying to free oneself from flypaper. But the important point here is that the Sarvastivadins relied on these twin dharmas of attainment and non-attainment to explain how dharmas could exist in the three periods of time, and thus how time could exist. Once we have attained or non-attained something, such attainment or non-attainment exists both as a seed in the past and as a fruit in the future. Thus, attainment and non-attainment are what make the present, the past, and the future entities of the mind possible. Without attainment or non-attainment there cannot be any dharmas.

Having saved these for last, Avalokiteshvara does not flinch but denies them both. Neither attainment nor non-attainment exists in emptiness. Not only do knowledge and the truths on which knowledge is based disappear, our attainment or non-attainment of any such knowledge or state of mind also disappears. And because they disappear, so does time. The past, the present, the future—all are fictions, sometimes useful sometimes not, but still fictions. And thus the entire matrix of the Sarvastivadin Abhidharma collapses. This concludes Avalokiteshvara's reinterpretation of this matrix in the light of the Prajnaparamita.

It should be noted that some Sanskrit texts omit *na-apraptih* (no non-attainment). This omission is reflected in some Chinese translations as well. However, to the extent that this section of the sutra is seen as a rebuttal of the Sarvastivadin Abhidharma, its omission leaves their conception of time intact. And it was their conception of time that distinguished the Sarvastivadin Abhidharma from those of all other sects. In the absence of no non-attainment, attainment becomes little more than an adjunct of knowledge. However, with both attainment and non-attainment denied, Avalokiteshvara prepares us for the bodhisattva, who relies on what is beyond knowledge, beyond attainment, and beyond non-attainment, namely, the Prajnaparamita.

Conze says, "By adding 'no knowledge,' somebody may have

wanted to make clear that in the dialectical logic of the Prajnaparamita a double negation does not make an affirmation. The
misconception might arise that 'the extinction of ignorance'
might be equivalent to a positive entity, named knowledge. The
addition of 'no knowledge' would guard against that misconception" (*Thirty Years of Buddhist Studies*, pp. 155–156).

Yin-shun says, "There is no truth outside of knowledge, and
there is no knowledge outside of truth."

Deva says, "What can see is knowledge. What is seen is attainment. Because suffering and happiness are forgotten, the mind
that knows does not arise. This is called attaining what is not
attained. This is complete attainment. It is not the same as mundane attainment. To counter the idea that bodhisattvas attain
anything, it says 'no knowledge and no attainment.'"

Fa-tsang says, "Not only are none of the previous dharmas
found in emptiness, the one who knows the knowledge of emptiness cannot be found either. Thus it says, 'no knowledge.' At
the same time, neither can this knowledge of emptiness that one
knows be found. Thus it says, 'no attainment.'"

Hui-chung says, "Examining dharmas and understanding
there is nothing to find is what we call knowledge. But since
dharmas are already empty, what need is there to examine them?
Thus, it says there is 'no knowledge.' And because our own
nature is pure and numinous and actually devoid of any dharma
that can be grasped, it also says there is 'no attainment.'"

Chen-k'o says, "Once the Five Skandhas are seen as empty,
the light of the mind shines alone. When all the clouds are gone,
the full moon fills the sky. Thus, birth and destruction, purity

and defilement, completeness and deficiency are all snowflakes on a red-hot stove. Once you realize true emptiness, how could the Five Skandhas alone be empty? The Twelve Abodes of Sensation, the Eighteen Elements of Perception, the Twelve Links of Dependent Origination, and the Four Noble Truths are all tortoise fur and rabbit horns. Ice doesn't melt by itself. It disappears when the sun comes out. Dharmas such as the Five Skandhas and Eighteen Elements of Perception and Twelve Links of Dependent Origination are like ice, and the illumination of prajna is like the sun. Once ice changes form, is it any different from a 'straw dog'? [cf. Lao-tzu's *Taoteching:* 5, where straw dogs, like Christmas trees, occupy a place of honor, but after the ceremony is over, they are thrown out with the trash]. Thus, it says 'no knowledge and no attainment.'"

Ching-mai says, "The foregoing has been for breaking through the attachments that arise from maintaining the reality of the skandhas and other categories, which emptiness was used to get rid of. Now, lest people think of emptiness as a state they finally attain, this too is eliminated. For emptiness is not a state that can be attained. It is like the hail that destroys crops. After the crops are flattened, the hail melts. If this was not the case, if people gave up existence only to grasp non-existence, it would be like trying to get off a mountain peak by jumping into a gorge. Disaster would be unavoidable."

Part Three

The Bodhisattva Path

21. THEREFORE, SHARIPUTRA, WITHOUT ATTAINMENT:
tasmac shariputra apraptitvad （舍利子)以無所得故

IN CONTRAST to the previous nine lines, which outline the shravaka path of early Buddhism only to reenvision it according to the Prajnaparamita, this and the following four lines summarize the career of the bodhisattva. Conze has suggested that these lines deal exclusively with the final stages of the bodhisattva path, which is more or less true, though they do begin at the beginning before they jump to the end. Descriptions of the bodhisattva path vary with the text, but among the landmarks near the end are the realization of the birthless nature of all dharmas, the absence of fear, and the decision not to enter nirvana.

Thus, while the shravaka path ends with no rebirth, the bodhisattva path ends with no birth, with the realization that nothing comes into existence in the first place. And because nothing arises, nothing ceases. And because nothing ceases, nothing is impermanent. And because nothing is impermanent, suffering cannot occur. And because suffering cannot occur, all beings are freed from suffering. And because all beings are freed from suffering, bodhisattvas fulfill their vow to liberate all beings. And because bodhisattvas fulfill their vow to liberate all beings, they themselves are liberated from liberating all beings. In the *Diamond Sutra* the Buddha presents the bodhisattva's vow in this manner: "In whatever conceivable realm of being one might conceive of beings, in the realm of complete nirvana I shall liberate them all. And though I thus liberate countless beings, not a single being is liberated" (3). Thus, the liberation of all beings revolves around the liberation of the bodhisattva from the concept of being. Only when bodhisattvas find no beings to liberate are they ready to complete the bodhisattva's path to buddhahood. But even at the end of the path, the problems of knowledge and attainment (as well as non-attainment) arise, just as they do on the shravaka path.

In the *Diamond Sutra* the Buddha asks Subhuti, "What do you think? Did the Tathagata realize any such dharma as unexcelled, perfect enlightenment?" Subhuti answers, "No, Bhagavan." And the Buddha concludes, "So it is. The slightest dharma is neither obtained nor found therein" (22). Not only are no beings liberated, no buddhahood is attained. Lao-tzu expresses a similar sentiment in his *Taoteching:* "Those who seek learning gain every day / those who seek the Way lose every day" (48).

22. BODHISATTVAS TAKE REFUGE IN PRAJNAPARAMITA:
bodhisattvo prajnaparamitam ashritya 菩薩依般若波羅蜜多

As noted earlier, the *Heart Sutra* is organized according to the sequence of categories in the Sarvastivadins' *Samyukt Agama*. This sutra now comes to that book's final category: the paragons of attainment. Or is it non-attainment? For bodhisattvas it is neither, for they have finally reached the point where neither attainment nor non-attainment has any meaning. Having transcended attainment (and non-attainment), they are now ready to begin the final stages of the bodhisattva path.

Bodhisattvas can be male or female, celibate or married. As long as they work toward enlightenment (*bodhi*) for themselves and liberation (*nirvana*) for others, they follow the bodhisattva path and are worthy of being called bodhisattvas. On the one hand, bodhisattvas include lay Buddhists whose practices are usually centered on acts of piety and devotion, and on the other, they include monks and nuns whose practices of austerity and meditation are beyond the reach of most mortals. While this would seem to represent a more egalitarian view of spiritual practice, it also represents a more demanding one (cf. Jan Nattier's translation and exposition of the *Ugra Paripriccha Sutra* in *A Few Good Men*). But however demanding such a path might be for some, the only qualification to walk it is the twofold vow to attain enlightenment and to liberate all beings. Of course, no one would or could make such a vow if they did not practice the Prajnaparamita. For without the Prajnaparamita, the vow is simply too overwhelming to attempt, much less fulfill. But once it is seen in the light of the Prajnaparamita, this vow is open to all, regardless of their capability or preferred form of practice. This is because the limiting categories of time and space disappear. Though it takes countless aeons to liberate all beings, the bodhisattva asks, "What aeons? What beings? What liberation?"

Avalokiteshvara is a bodhisattva at the end of the bodhisattva path, someone for whom time and space have disappeared. But he begins his summary of the path at the beginning, with taking refuge, which is the first step. Normally, Buddhists take refuge in the Three Treasures: the Buddha, the Dharma, and the Sangha, the teacher, the teaching, and the community of those taught. This is all that is urged of anyone who travels the Buddhist path. Taking refuge in the Buddha, we learn to transform anger into compassion; taking refuge in the Dharma, we learn to transform delusion into wisdom; and taking refuge in the Sangha, we learn to transform desire into generosity. Because anger and desire arise from delusion, the most important of the Three Treasures is the Dharma and thus the cultivation of wisdom. Buddhas come and go, as do communities of fellow practitioners. But the Dharma is not subject to the limitations of space, time, or conception. Thus, bodhisattvas begin by taking refuge in Prajnaparamita, the wisdom that is the mother of all buddhas, and which is another name for the *dharma-kaya*, the embodiment of the Dharma.

In addition to taking refuge in the Three Treasures, monks and nuns and lay practitioners agree to abide by certain precepts in regulating their conduct, such as not killing, not stealing, not lying, not engaging in sexual misconduct, and not using intoxicants. In the case of bodhisattvas, this list of negative prohibitions is amended to include the more positive injunctions of the Six Paramitas, or Perfections: generosity, morality, forbearance, vigor, meditation, and wisdom. Here, the bodhisattva's refuge is in wisdom alone, as it includes the other five paramitas. However, the word *paramita*, as noted at the beginning of this commentary, distinguishes this wisdom as different from other

forms of wisdom. This wisdom is "transcendent." Thus, bodhisattvas know that all dharmas are marked with emptiness and
that there is nothing to attain or not to attain. And realizing
there is nothing to attain or not to attain, they take refuge in
this realization. Anything less would be unworthy of a bodhisattva. Actually, anything less would be impossible. For a bodhisattva, there is nothing else to rely on.

23. AND LIVE WITHOUT WALLS OF THE MIND:
viharaty acitta-avaranah 故心無罣礙

The refuge of Prajnaparamita is a refuge without walls. Buddhists recognize three barriers (*avarana*) to spiritual growth:
walls of karma (*karma-avarana*), which include all limiting cir-
cumstances; walls of passion (*klesha-avarana*), which include
anger and desire; and walls of knowledge (*jneya-avarana*), which
include all forms of delusion, namely, the belief that something
exists when it does not or that something does not exist when
it does. Here, Avalokiteshvara uses "walls of the mind" (*citta-
avarana*) as inclusive of all three but also to stress that such barriers are self-imposed. These are the barriers that emptiness
dissolves. Commenting on this obstruction-less state, Conze
says, "It may either be described as an object without a subject,
or a subject without an object. When viewed as an object without a subject, it is called 'Suchness.' When viewed from the sub-
ject-side, the transcendental reality is known as 'Thought-only'"
(*Buddhist Wisdom Books*, pp. 95–96). In several Sanskrit editions
of the *Heart Sutra*, *citta-avarana* is replaced by *citta-alambana*,

"objects of the mind." Although it comes to the same thing, there is not much support for this variation.

Hui-chung says, "As long as there is the slightest dharma, there is an obstruction. But the mind and the world are empty. No matter how we think or act, nothing at all happens. How could there be an obstruction?"

Pao-t'ung says, "For someone with no mind, there is still a barrier. What do I mean? A white cloud blocks the valley mouth. Returning birds can't find the way to their nests."

Ching-mai says, "The absence of walls explains how the liberation door of emptiness works. This means by understanding that dharmas are empty inside and out, the vision of one's wisdom is not blocked by the nature of existence."

24. WITHOUT WALLS OF THE MIND AND THUS WITHOUT FEARS: *citta-avarana nastitvad atrasto* 無罣礙故無有恐怖

Dwelling without walls, bodhisattvas see "things as it is," to quote Shunryu Suzuki (cf. *Not Always So*). We fear what we cannot see. Once the walls with which we have surrounded ourselves are gone, we see the indivisibility of things, we see the light. In the light of Prajnaparamita, bodhisattvas realize the birthlessness of dharmas. And once they are able to endure such a realization, there is nothing left to fear. Fearlessness is characteristic of the eighth stage of the bodhisattva path, which is essentially the last stage, as the ninth and tenth stages concern buddhahood. Our fear begins with our separation from emptiness. And it ends with our reunion.

Among the many fears that assail us, and there is one for every wall in the cities of our minds, there are five that are said to concern beginning bodhisattvas: the fear of survival (that we will not be able to survive if we practice generosity); the fear of criticism (that we will not be able to endure the criticism of associating with disreputable people while trying to liberate all beings); the fear of death (that we will not be able to give up our lives to help others); the fear of a bad existence (that we will be born during a time when the Dharma is not taught); and the fear of speaking before an assembly (that we will embarrass ourselves or fail to teach others).

Hui-chung says, "There is nothing to grasp in the mind. So what is there to seek? If you can't find the mind, who is it who gives rise to fear? Thus it says, 'without fears.'"

Te-ch'ing says, "All dharmas are basically empty. But someone who relies on sentience or discrimination to view such things will become hopelessly entangled by the mind and its objects. Whereas someone who relies on the true wisdom of prajna will see that the mind and its objects are empty. And instead of obstructions, they will only meet with freedom. And because their minds are free of walls, there is nothing to fear from birth and death. And because there is nothing to fear from birth and death, there is also no buddhahood to seek. It is because of the fear of birth and death that we seek nirvana. But this is nothing but a dream or delusion."

Ching-mai says, "Having no walls and thus no fears explains the liberation door of formlessness. Once a person realizes dharmas are empty both inside and out, they know dharmas have no form. Unless they know dharmas have no form, they will be blocked outside and subject to countless fears inside. But once they realize dharmas have no form, they won't be blocked outside and won't find anything to fear inside."

25. THEY SEE THROUGH DELUSIONS AND FINALLY NIRVANA: *viparyasa atikranto nishtha nirvanah*
遠離顛倒夢想究竟涅槃

The word *viparyasa* refers to what is upside-down, what is contrary to the way things are. In Buddhism this refers specifically to four delusions: claiming something is permanent that is not permanent, claiming something is pleasurable that is not pleasurable, claiming something is self-existent that is not self-existent, and claiming something is pure that is not pure. These four views of permanence, pleasure, self-existence, and purity are used by people to establish the reality of the mundane world, the world of sansara, the world of birth and death. Such views were considered to be mistaken by all early sects of Buddhism, but only with regard to the conditioned dharmas of sansara—conditioned dharmas being those subject to cause and effect. With regard to the unconditioned dharma of nirvana, the opposite was held to be true and to hold otherwise was thought to be equally mistaken.

Since this sutra is a critique of the views of the Sarvastivadins in particular and other early Buddhist sects in general, Avalokiteshvara includes under "delusions" not only the four views of the mundane world but also the four views of those early sects that maintained nirvana was permanent, pleasurable, self-existent, and pure. Thus, bodhisattvas not only see through (*atikranto*) delusions concerning the existence of sansara, they also see through delusions concerning the existence of nirvana. But this is not all. Bodhisattvas also see through delusions concerning the non-existence of nirvana, for existence and non-existence are terms in a dialectic that does not apply to what is beyond all duality.

Several copies of the longer version of the *Heart Sutra* add the verb *prapta* (attain) at the end of the phrase *nishtha nirvana* (finally nirvana). Conze also included it in his Sanskrit edition of 1948/1957 (cf. *Buddhist Wisdom Books*), but he deleted it in his second edition in 1967 (cf. *Thirty Years of Buddhist Studies*). Other translators and commentators, either aware of this variant or thinking it must be implied, have taken this phrase to mean something equivalent to "finally attain nirvana." But this would amount to the attainment of something that cannot be attained and would contradict Avalokiteshvara's earlier statement in line 20 that there is "no knowledge, no attainment and no non-attainment." To avoid this problem, I have read both *viparyasa* (delusion) and *nishtha-nirvana* (finally nirvana) as objects of the verb *atikranto* (see through), which is allowed by the vagaries of Sanskrit grammar in the absence of *prapta*. Thus, bodhisattvas do not reach or attain nirvana but overcome all delusions, including those that concern the ultimate goal of nirvana, namely, views that see nirvana as either permanent or not permanent, pleasurable or not pleasurable, self-existent or not self-existent, pure or not pure. Nirvana is simply the final delusion.

Thus, Mahayana sutras never tire of telling us that bodhisattvas do not attain nirvana and even avoid it, that their goal is elsewhere, namely the liberation of all beings. This is also the view of the *Perfection of Wisdom in Twenty-five Thousand Lines*, which states that while bodhisattvas lead others to nirvana, nirvana itself is a dream or delusion. And in Chapter Two of the *Lotus Sutra*, the Buddha tells Shariputra and the other arhans seeking to become bodhisattvas that the nirvana they have attained is really but an imaginary oasis on the road to buddhahood.

As for the word *nirvana*, there are several explanations of its origin. The usual derivation is to interpret it as a combination of *nir* (a negative prefix) and either *va*, meaning "blow," or *van*, meaning "desire." Thus, *nir-vana* means "the cessation of breath" or "the cessation of desire." Sanskrit etymologists, however, have dug much deeper and have extracted such diverse meanings from *vana* as the "path" of transmigration, the "stench" of defilement, the "forest" of the skandhas, and the "thread" of karma (cf. *Mahavibhasha Shastra*: 32). When Buddhist monks first began translating Sanskrit texts into Chinese, they tried dozens of equivalents for *nirvana* before finally giving up and simply transcribing the term, thus allowing it to take on different meanings depending on the context.

Another common derivation was to understand *nirvana* as a combination of the negative prefix *nir* and the root *vri*, "to cover," "to restrain," or "to obstruct." This is most likely the sense understood here, with *nir-vana* referring to "no walls of the mind," as the word for "walls," *avarana*, is also derived from *vri*. Thus, not only do bodhisattvas see through delusions of existence and non-existence, they see through delusions of having stepped past all such delusions. In other Prajnaparamita texts, such as the *Ratnagunasancaya Gatha*, the term *nir-vriti*, based on the same derivation, is used to describe that state into which bodhisattvas do not retire, for bodhisattvas vow to remain in sansara until all beings are liberated.

In the *Samyukt Agama*, Jamburatha asks Shariputra, "You speak of nirvana. But what is nirvana?" And Shariputra answers, "Nirvana is the permanent cessation of desire, the permanent cessation of anger, the permanent cessation of ignorance, the permanent cessation of all passions. This is what is meant by 'nirvana.'" And Jamburatha asks again, "Is there a path, a direction, a practice or set of practices that leads to nirvana?" And Shariputra answers, "There is. It is called the Eightfold Noble Path, from Right Views to Right Meditation" (1478).

Fa-tsang says, "Outside, they have no fear of demons or injustice, thus evil conditions cease. Inside, they have no confusion of doubts or obstructions, thus evil causes stop. Nirvana is perfect peace. 'Perfect' means complete in every virtue. 'Peace' means free of every obstruction. Wisdom is able to plumb the very limits of nirvana."

Hui-chung says, "To look for something outside the mind or to see emptiness inside the mind is to be mistaken. To imagine something exists when it does not is to dream. What the mind depends upon are views. When you suddenly realize the source of the mind, there is nothing at all to grasp. Thus it says to 'see through all delusions.'"

Deva says, "The delusions people cling to are like the image of water in a fire, flowers in the sky, like fur on a tortoise or horns on a rabbit or like the child of a barren woman. Worldly desires, wealth, fame, and position are all like this. Fools think they are real. Those who are wise understand they are dreamlike conceptions and empty illusions and that their original nature is not apparent. Whatever is apparent is the result of delusion."

Ching-mai says, "This explains the liberation door of no desire. Once one realizes dharmas have no nature, and they aren't blocked outside and have no fears inside, they come to know that dharmas are simply delusions, like dreams, and are false and not real. Thus, they see through them and don't give rise to desires."

26/27. ALL BUDDHAS PAST, PRESENT AND FUTURE / ALSO TAKE REFUGE IN PRAJNAPARAMITA: *tryadhva vyavasthitah sarva-buddhah prajnaparamitam ashritya*

三世諸佛，依般若波羅蜜多

As noted above, bodhisattvas see through the delusion of nirvana and thus the delusion of putting an end to their sansaric existence. Instead of nirvana, they take refuge in Prajnaparamita. For it is from the womb of Prajnaparamita that buddhas are born, which is why Prajnaparamita is called *buddha-matri*, the Mother of Buddhas. As the Buddha says in the *Diamond Sutra*, "From this is born the unexcelled, perfect enlightenment of tathagatas, arhans, and fully enlightened ones. From this are born buddhas and bhagavans" (8). Here, Avalokiteshvara reminds us of this process, that buddhas become buddhas by taking refuge in Prajnaparamita and not by attaining nirvana. In truth, they have nowhere else to go, for they have been left without even a speck of dust to stand on. Thus, by taking refuge in Prajnaparamita, they enter the womb of Prajnaparamita and await their rebirth as buddhas.

Deva says, "'Buddha' is Sanskrit for 'awakened,' to awaken oneself and awaken others."

Fa-tsang says, "The buddhas of the past, present, and future take no other road and use only this gate."

Ching-chueh says, "Although we say the nirmana-kaya (manifestation body of a buddha) exists in three periods of time, in reality the past and future are without limit. The *Tuchenglun Inscription* says, 'The nature of a tathagata is pure and not different in the three periods.' Another commentary says, 'The dharma-kaya [real body of a buddha] is pure, like the moon in the sky, and the sanbhoga-kaya [a buddha's body of realization] is an empty image, like a reflection on the water. A reflection on the water is not the object itself, but being visible, it can lead us to the object, which is the moon in the sky. The sanbhoga-kaya is an empty image, but although it isn't real, being visible, it can lead us to what is real, which is the pure dharma-kaya.'"

Hui-chung says, "All vexation, ignorance, passion, and delusion of the past, the present and the future are fundamentally pure. Thus it says 'all buddhas of the past, present and future.' Because they realize fundamental wisdom without becoming attached to anything, it says they 'take refuge in Prajnaparamita.'"

Chen-k'o says, "Buddhas and ordinary people aren't really different. Buddhas are simply people who are free of birth and

death, love and hate, while ordinary people aren't free of birth or
death, love or hate."

28. AND REALIZE UNEXCELLED, PERFECT ENLIGHTENMENT:
anuttaran samyak sambodhim abhisambuddhah
故得阿耨多羅三藐三菩提

The expression "unexcelled, perfect enlightenment" goes back
to the earliest scriptures of the Sarvastivadins as well as those
of the Sthaviravadins (Theravadins) and was apparently first
used by the Buddha. It was said that the addition of qualifiers
such as *anuttara* (unexcelled) and *samyak* (perfect) was meant
to distinguish the enlightenment (*sambodhi*) of a buddha from
that of other sects. But it was also meant to distinguish the
enlightenment of bodhisattvas from that of shravakas and pratyeka-buddhas.

   As it surpasses the understanding of those limited by concepts, it is called "unexcelled." Since it is more complete than
the understanding of those limited by reason, it is called "perfect." And because it dispels the darkness of ignorance and shadows of delusion, it is called "enlightenment" (*sambodhi*). In the
Sanskrit word for "enlightenment," the prefix *sam* means "complete" and was added as an intensifier to *bodhi*, which by itself
also means "enlightenment." The verb here is *abhi-sam-buddha*,
in which *abhi-sam* means "to reach completely," and *buddha*
means "awareness," which I have summarized with "to realize."
This is the fruit of the seed cultivated by Avalokiteshvara at the
beginning of this sutra where he looks upon the Five Skandhas

and sees that they, and all other dharmas, are empty of self-existence. Thus, if the seed is empty, so is the fruit.

In the *Diamond Sutra*, the Buddha says, "Subhuti, undifferentiated is this dharma in which nothing is differentiated. Thus is it called 'unexcelled, perfect enlightenment.' Without a self, without a being, without a life, without a soul, undifferentiated is this unexcelled, perfect enlightenment by means of which all auspicious dharmas are realized. And how so? Auspicious dharmas, Subhuti, 'auspicious dharmas' are spoken of by the Tathagata as 'no dharmas.' Thus are they called 'auspicious dharmas'" (23).

In the *Vimalakirti Sutra*, when the deva in Vimalakirti's room tells Shariputra that attaining unexcelled, perfect enlightenment is impossible, because enlightenment cannot be grasped, Shariputra says, "But what does it mean then when we are told that buddhas as numerous as the sands of the Ganges attain, have attained, and will attain unexcelled, perfect enlightenment?" And the deva replies, "Shariputra, to say that there are three periods of time is simply a conventional way of talking. It does not mean that enlightenment exists in the past, the present, or the future" (7).

Hui-chung says, "If you believe in this unsurpassed, true Tao, your mind is already the buddha. Thus it says they realize 'unexcelled, perfect enlightenment.'"

Te-ch'ing says, "Not only do bodhisattvas rely on this prajna for their practice, there is no buddha in the past, the present, or the future who does not rely on this prajna in order to realize unexcelled, perfect enlightenment."

Part Four

The Womb of Buddhas

---

29. YOU SHOULD THEREFORE KNOW THE GREAT
MANTRA OF PRAJNAPARAMITA: *tasmaj jnatavyan
prajnaparamita maha-mantro* 故知般若波羅蜜多是大神咒

B Y TAKING REFUGE in Prajnaparamita, bodhisattvas overcome all obstacles to enlightenment.
With the way now clear, Avalokiteshvara shows
us the door to the *sanctum sanctorum*.

In line 20, we are told that in emptiness there is "no knowledge" (*na jnana*). So how can we now know (*jnatavyan*) this
mantra? Unlike such dharmas as the skandhas, the abodes, the
elements, the links, or the truths regarding suffering, this mantra
is not an entity of the mind. We can know this mantra because
it involves no knowledge, rather it leads beyond knowledge.
This is the only form of knowledge cultivated by a bodhisattva.
The knowledge of dharmas turns out to be no knowledge, and
the knowledge of no knowledge turns out to be the only knowledge worth knowing.

Mantras are knowledge that transcends our normal understanding of knowledge. They are the creation of beings in touch
with the underlying vibrations of the mind and the keys that

unlock its power through sympathetic harmonics. In the Chungnan Mountains south of Sian, I once met a Buddhist master who had founded four Buddhist colleges before finally retiring to spend her last years in a mountain hut. She told me in all seriousness that mantras were taught to humans by beings from another world. No doubt their authors were from another world. At the very least, it was a world whose origin stretches back to India's pre-Vedic, pre-historic past, when the only knowledge worthy of the name was knowledge of ritual, and at the heart of every ritual was a mantra. In the Buddha's day, mantras were in widespread use among almost all religious practitioners, including his own disciples. Although the Buddha sometimes criticized their use, as in the *Dhirgha Agama* (14), he also taught them to his disciples for such purposes as protection from snakes, as in the *Samyukt Agama* (9). In this regard, the Buddha distinguished between mantras that simply conferred magic powers and those that provided protection or spiritual aid.

Often a distinction is made between mantras and dharanis, whereby mantras are said to be strings of one or more syllables not meant to be understood as human language, and dharanis are said to be intelligible summaries of some profound truth. But this is a late distinction, and early texts use the words *mantra* and *dharani* in reference to both intelligible and unintelligible incantations. Since this sutra uses the word *mantra*, and the sutra itself was often referred to as a *dharani*, it was most likely composed before such a distinction was made.

Andre Padoux says, "a mantra has a use rather than a meaning" (*Understanding Mantras*, p. 302). This mantra, however, has both. It contains the essential teaching of the Prajnaparamita and also enables those who chant it to join the lineage of buddhas who have their origin in this teaching. In his commentary, Vajrapani says, "The mantra of the Perfection of Wisdom is not a mantra for pacification, increase, power, or wrath. What is it? By merely understanding the meaning of this mantra, the mind is freed" (Donald Lopez, *Elaborations on Emptiness*, p. 213).

A mantra is like a magic lamp. If you rub it correctly, its resident genie will appear. During Hsuan-tsang's stay in India (630–644), he once traveled through Andra Pradesh and came to a cavern where the monk Bhavaviveka lived during the previous century and where he was said to have chanted a mantra every day for three years in order to invoke the appearance of Avalokiteshvara. The resident genie of this mantra, however, is not Avalokiteshvara, but Prajnaparamita, the Goddess of Transcendent Wisdom and the Mother of All Buddhas, and it turns out she is already present. Thus, bodhisattvas who know this mantra know their mother.

Ching-chueh says, "Once you catch a fish, you can forget the trap. Once you catch a rabbit, you can forget the snare. Once you catch the meaning, you can forget the words. The *Pravara-deva-raja Paripriccha Sutra* says, 'Though words are used to express a dharani, a dharani has no words. The great compassionate power of prajna is beyond words and expressions.'"

30. THE MANTRA OF GREAT MAGIC:
maha-vidya mantro 是大明咒

The word *vidya* is derived from *vid*, "to understand," and includes every kind of mastery from science to practical arts to magic. Among Buddhists, the term *vidya* is often used as equivalent to the word *mantra* because it, too, encapsulates a system of mastery, though one that surpasses the ken of ordinary mortals. But *vidya* is also distinguished from *mantra* as referring to the mastery of female deities, while *mantra* refers to that of male deities. Thus, the term *mahavidya* (great master/magician) has become an appellation for many of India's most popular goddesses, including Kali, Tara, Durga, Sarasvati, and Lakshmi (cf. *Tantric Visions of the Divine Feminine: The Ten Mahavidyas*, by David Kinsley, pp. 57–60). The reason for such usage is that mantras (or vidyas) have the power to give birth to a new state of consciousness. Thus, each of these *mahavidyas* is associated with a particular form of spiritual awareness and only appears when her mantra is chanted, just as a genie only appears when its magic lamp is rubbed. But not all mantras give rise to such deities, only mantras that possess great magic. In this case, the mantra does not give rise to Prajnaparamita but becomes her womb and thus the source of the greatest of all magic, the appearance of a buddha.

The word *mantra* means "protector of thought." Thus, a mantra is like an amulet or talisman, but one that protects its user's mind rather than their body. Normally, mantras are only efficacious when transmitted from teacher to disciple during a carefully ritualized ceremony in which the proper pronunciation is taught along with instructions concerning accompanying gestures, postures, or religious paraphernalia. But the *Heart Sutra* mantra, being also a dharani, is not subject to such restrictions. It is not secret but accessible to all who have the good fortune to encounter it. The word *dharani* means "to call to mind." Like a memento, it reminds us of the teaching we have resolved to practice. But it is much more than that. It is also our guide. Thus, a mantra contains the protective deity, and a dharani leads us into her sanctuary. In this case, the *Heart Sutra* mantra does both.

In some perfection of wisdom texts, such as the *Perfection of Wisdom in One Hundred Thousand Lines*, the word *mantra* is replaced by *vidya* in sections of text identical to lines 29–32, in which case this line would read the "magic of great magic" or the "mastery of great mastery," and the remaining lines would also substitute "magic" or "mastery" for "mantra."

31. THE UNEXCELLED MANTRA: *anuttara mantro* 是無上咒

The term *anuttara* (unexcelled) is a title of every buddha and is taken from the phrase *anuttara samyak sambodhi,* "unexcelled, perfect enlightenment." Enlightenment is called "unexcelled" because it goes beyond all categories, including the higher categories of the Abhidharma. And because this mantra is identical to enlightenment, it, too, is called "unexcelled." There is nothing beyond it. It is the beyond.

This same series of epithets also occurs in Kumarajiva's translation of the *Perfection of Wisdom in Twenty-five Thousand Lines*, where Indra, who rules the heaven in which the Buddha's mother was reborn, sighs, "Bhagavan, the Prajnaparamita is a mantra of great magic, an unexcelled mantra, a mantra equal to the unequalled. And why is this? Because, Bhagavan, the Prajnaparamita can eliminate all evil dharmas and give rise to all good dharmas." To this the Buddha assents, then adds, "All buddhas of the past have relied on this mantra to realize unexcelled, perfect enlightenment. And all the buddhas of the future and all the buddhas of the present throughout the ten directions also rely on this mantra to realize unexcelled, perfect enlightenment. It is because of this mantra that the world knows the Path" (Chinese Tripitaka, vol. 8, p. 286b–c).

32. THE MANTRA EQUAL TO THE UNEQUALLED: *asama-sama mantrah* 是無等等咒

The term *asama-sama* (equal to the unequalled) is another title of every buddha. Because this mantra is identical to enlightenment, it is the equal of every buddha. Thus, it is equal to the unequalled. On those occasions when the Buddha was asked if he could suggest a comparison for buddhahood, he pointed to the sky, unbounded, indivisible, and all-pervasive. Being unexcelled, this mantra likewise has nothing above it. Being unequalled, this mantra has nothing below it. And being equal to the unequalled, it is no different from the buddhahood of every buddha. Buddhas differ, but not their buddhahood. Thus, this mantra is known by all buddhas, just as children know their mother.

In Kumarajiva's translation of the *Perfection of Wisdom in Twenty-five Thousand Lines*, Shariputra and the other members of the assembly address the Buddha: "In practicing the Prajna-paramita equal to the unequalled in their giving, bodhisattvas perfect the paramita of generosity equal to the unequalled and obtain a body equal to the unequalled and a dharma equal to the unequalled, namely, unexcelled, perfect enlightenment. The same is true for the paramitas of morality, forbearance, vigor, meditation, and wisdom. The Bhagavan has also practiced this Prajna-paramita and perfected the Six Paramitas equal to the unequalled and obtained a dharma equal to the unequalled and obtained a form equal to the unequalled, and sensations, perceptions, memories, and consciousness equal to the unequalled and has turned the Wheel of Dharma equal to the unequalled. And so it has been for buddhas of the past" (Chinese Tripitaka, vol. 8, p. 229c).

Te-ch'ing says, "Because it can drive away the demonic torment of birth and death, it is called 'the great mantra'; because it can break through the ignorance and darkness of the endless night of birth and death, it is called 'the mantra of great magic'; because no dharma in this or any other world excels prajna, it is called 'the unexcelled mantra'; because prajna is the mother of buddhas and gives birth to limitless virtues, nothing in this or in any world can match it, while it alone can match everything else. Hence, it is called 'the mantra equal to the unequalled.'"

Hui-chung says, "A mantra has many meanings. It can't be fully explained to people that their own minds have no limits and that they come and go without obstruction and yet never move. This is why this is called a 'great mantra.' Because the mind is basically pure and clear and dwells forever in the perfect illumination of what is real and responds to what is present without becoming exhausted, it is a 'mantra of great magic.' And because none of the myriad dharmas is beyond the mind, and nothing surpasses it, it is an 'unexcelled mantra.' And because the word 'mind' cannot be characterized as existing or not existing and is without limits, borders, or comparisons, it is a 'mantra equal to the unequalled.'"

Fa-tsang says, "It eliminates obstructions and is not false, hence it is called 'great.' It is the light of wisdom and not ignorance, hence it is called 'magic.' It is surpassed by nothing else, hence it is called 'unexcelled.' And it has no peer, hence it is called 'equal to the unequalled.' But why not simply say it is 'unequalled'? Because it appears to be the equal of enlightenment."

Ming-k'uang says, "According to the principles of the Four Teachings, the 'great mantra' is the Hinayana Teaching of the Four Truths regarding what is born and what dies; the 'mantra of great magic' is the Common Teaching of the Four Truths regarding what is neither born nor dies; the 'unexcelled mantra' is the Special Teaching of the Four Truths regarding what is infinite; and the 'mantra equal to the unequalled' is the Complete Teaching of the Four Truths regarding what is unconditioned."

33. WHICH HEALS ALL SUFFERING AND IS TRUE, NOT FALSE: *sarva-duhkha prashamanah satyam amithyatvat* 能除一切苦真實不虛

Here, Avalokiteshvara reveals the function of this mantra as well as its qualification to fulfill that function. Its function is to free us from suffering. Its qualification is that it is true.

The Buddha often told his disciples that everything he taught them could be summed up by the Four Truths: suffering, the origin of suffering, the end of suffering, and the path leading to the end of suffering. Thus, at the conclusion of this sutra, Avalokiteshvara returns to the beginning: suffering and the way out of suffering.

Buddhists recognize eight kinds of suffering: the suffering of birth, the suffering of age, the suffering of illness, the suffering of death, the suffering of separation from what one loves, the suffering of meeting what one hates, the suffering of not getting what one wants, and the suffering of the skandhas. Avalokiteshvara tells Shariputra that in emptiness there is no suffering, no source of suffering, no relief from suffering, and no path leading out of suffering. But to keep Shariputra from treating this insight as another level of intellectual understanding, which was the skill for which he was best known, Avalokiteshvara directs him instead to this mantra, which heals our suffering by bringing Shariputra, and us along with him, face-to-face with the true nature of suffering. The Sanskrit verb here is *prashamana*. In addition to "heal," it means to "calm."

It has become a commonplace to say "the truth will set you free." But no one has ever been freed by the truths of this world. Thus, this mantra does not represent a conventional truth or a provisional truth of some lesser path that only applies under certain conditions to certain persons. Rather it represents a truth beyond which we need no further instruction. Such a claim borders on the presumptuous. Hence, Avalokiteshvara insists on its validity.

Deva says, "This sutra can put an end to the turning wheel of birth and death. It is like a bright lamp that can dispel darkness, like a wonderful medicine that can eliminate poison, and like tweezers that can extract a cataract from the eye. Essentially, it is like a magic pearl that grants to its possessor whatever they seek or wish for."

Fa-tsang says, "Because there is no doubt that it eliminates suffering, it is said to be 'true, not false.'"

Hui-chung says, "By relying on this mantra, the minds of all buddhas transcend the Three Realms and are not subject to the round of existence. Thus it says it can 'heal all suffering.' Because it points directly to your mind as absolutely the buddha and as not requiring cultivation or realization, it says it is 'true.' Because the mind is not an incarnated body and is free of confusion and always at peace, it says it is 'not false.'"

34. THE MANTRA IN PRAJNAPARAMITA SPOKEN THUS:
prajnaparamitayam ukto mantrah tadyatha
說般若波羅蜜多咒即說咒曰

The operative term here is "in." This mantra is in Prajnaparamita because it is her womb, which she creates through its sound and which we enter through sympathetic harmonics when we chant it. Some mothers sing lullabies. Prajnaparamita sings this mantra. The reason Avalokiteshvara knows this mantra is that he is a subsequent incarnation of Maya, the mother of Shakyamuni, and thus a manifestation of Prajnaparamita, the Mother of

All Buddhas. In Vajrayana Buddhism, Avalokiteshvara is also known as the *vidya-adhipati*, "bestower of spells."

In ancient India, cosmic order was maintained by the practice of *rita*, or ritual, and the heart of every ritual involved the incantation of a series of potent sounds, sometimes meaningful, sometimes not, but invariably directed toward a deva whose assistance was sought. In this case, we are not directing this mantra toward a deva but toward reality itself, as personified by the goddess Prajnaparamita. David Kinsley says, "It is not that the mantra *belongs to* the goddess, which is the way one is often tempted to understand the relationship between the deity and the mantra; the situation, rather, is that the mantra *is* the goddess" (*Tantric Visions of the Divine Feminine*, p. 58). In this case I would say that the mantra is not the goddess *per se* but her womb.

Hui-chung says, "A mantra is simply a person's own mind. Because these words point to the mind, it is called the mantra of 'Prajnaparamita.'"

Te-ch'ing says, "The foregoing text is exoteric prajna. This mantra is esoteric prajna. There's no place for an intellectual understanding, only silent repetition. The speed of its effectiveness depends upon the inconceivable power of forgetting feelings and putting an end to understanding. But the reason behind the speed of its effectiveness is the light inherent in everyone's mind. Buddhas realize it and use it to perform miraculous feats and wonders. Ordinary beings mistake it and use it to create delusion and trouble. They use it without being aware of it because they remain blind to what is real. Thus, they suffer in vain. Is this not a pity? But if they could wake up right now to what they already possess and turn their light inward and focus their minds on cultivation, the barrier of birth and death would suddenly break apart, just as a single lamp dispels the gloom in a room that has been dark for a thousand years. One doesn't need any other method. If we resolve to escape from birth and death and then abandon this, we will be without a boat or raft. Thus it is said that in the ever-surging sea of suffering, prajna serves as our raft. And during the long night of ignorance, prajna serves as our lamp. People race down precipitous paths, or they drift in a perilous sea and are content in their obliviousness. Who knows where they will end up? Prajna is also like a miraculous sword. It cuts people in two without them even feeling it. Who but the wise can use it? Certainly not those with small minds."

35. 'GATE GATE, PARAGATE, PARASANGATE, BODHI SVAHA'
揭帝揭帝，般羅揭帝，般羅僧揭帝，菩提僧莎

In ancient India, many schools of thought maintained, or at least paid homage to the idea, that sound vibrations are the ultimate constituents of reality. Thus, in order to preserve the spiritual potency of this mantra, those who have translated this sutra have preferred to transliterate or transcribe the mantra's Sanskrit sounds into their respective written systems. Indian and Tibetan commentators have sometimes added the syllable *om* to the beginning of this mantra, apparently to balance the *svaha* at the end and to set this off as sacred space. However, *om* appears in only a handful of Sanskrit copies and is not present in any early translation, other than that of the Tantric master Amoghavajra (705–774). Hence, I have not included it. It should also be noted that this mantra appears in slightly different form in two other sutras translated into Chinese in the fifth and sixth centuries, and it is also listed in a seventh-century catalogue of mantras, suggesting its potency was recognized long before Hsuan-tsang encountered it.

As for the meaning of the words that make up the mantra, *gate* is normally written *gata*, as in *tatha-gata*, in which case it is a past passive participle of *gam* (to go, to understand) and means "gone" or "understood." But since it does not appear as *gata* in any Sanskrit copy of the *Heart Sutra*, the author must have had something else in mind. There are several possible readings that result from replacing the *a* with an *e*. As *gate*, it can be read as a feminine vocative ("O you—the goddess Prajnaparamita, I presume—who have gone / understood") or as a locative absolute ("when gone / understood"). These two possibilities were noted by Conze, but he overlooked a third. *Gate* can also be read as a simple locative masculine ("into the gone / understanding"). Given the interpretation of this mantra as equivalent to the womb of Prajnaparamita, the locative masculine, leading us into her womb, is clearly preferable. Compared with this third possibility, which involves our active participation in this incantation, the feminine vocative seems primarily devotional, and the locative absolute overly abstract. Of course, the choice of *gate* over *gata* may have nothing to do with meaning. It may simply come down to the author's awareness of the difference in the power of the two sounds. Or it could be both.

The remaining words of the mantra tell us more about the "gone" or the "understanding" into which we are entering. *Para* means "beyond." Thus, *para-gate* means "into the gone beyond" or "into the understanding beyond." And *para-san-gate* means "into the gone completely beyond" or "into the understanding completely beyond." Thus, the word around which this mantra, and the entire sutra, revolves is "beyond." After negating the categories of the Abhidharma, this sutra refuses to set up another category or set of categories. Whatever it is, this teaching is beyond it, including itself. This is the function of this mantra: to go beyond language and the categories in which language imprisons us and to lead us into the womb of Prajna-paramita, which is the Gone, the Gone Beyond, the Gone Completely Beyond.

The mantra concludes with *bodhi svaha*. While the first part of the mantra leads us into the womb, this last part gives us birth. *Bodhi*, which is case-free here and thus the magic seed of our rebirth, means "enlightenment," and *svaha* is exclamatory: "at last," "amen," "hallelujah." It was used at the end of Vedic rituals while making oblations to the gods and thus has the function of consecrating an offering.

Having been left without a path to follow since line 19, Indian commentators, writing long after this sutra first appeared, have tried to find in the words of the mantra the five stages of practice as they conceived them in such texts as the *Abhisamay-alankara*: accumulation, preparation, vision, meditation, and transcendence. Such commentators have then read back into the sutra these same five phases of progression. Lopez says, "This is the fantasy of the *Heart Sutra*'s mantra. It is imagined as a supplement to the sutra, augmenting it by adding a path to the proclamation of emptiness, by fulfilling emptiness, while at the same time displacing the sutra" (*Elaborations on Emptiness*, p. 185). The *Heart Sutra* teaches many lessons and satisfies many interpretations, and I wouldn't want to deny anything that works. But putting this mantra in a cage is not as good as setting it free.

Fa-tsang says, "There are two meanings to this mantra. First, it can't be explained. This is because it is the secret language of buddhas and not dependent on one's level of understanding. One simply chants or calls it to mind, and it eliminates obstructions and increases one's blessings and does not need an explanation. Second, if we insist on an explanation, *gate* means 'gone' or to 'ferry across,' which is the effect of deep wisdom. The repetition of *gate* means to 'ferry oneself and also ferry others.' *Paragate* means 'the other shore,' which is the place one is ferried to. And the *san* in *parasangate* means 'together,' 'everyone ferried across together.' *Bodhi* tells us what kind of 'other shore,' namely that of enlightenment. And *svaha* means 'right now.'"

Hui-chung says, "A mantra like this points directly at the mind. Because it is neither moving nor still, you can't use the mind to find the mind. Because the mind has no beginning or end, you can't use the mind to put an end to the mind. Because there's no inside, outside, or in between, if you look for the mind, there's no place to find it. If there's no place to find it, then you can't find it. Therefore, you should realize there is no mind at all. And because there is no mind at all, demon realms can't affect you. And because you can't be affected, you subdue all demons. The sutras say, 'Subduing demons is the place of enlightenment.' Because you don't waver, when you look at people who don't understand their own mind, you can use this to cure their illnesses. If you see dharmas outside the mind, demon realms will appear before you, and your mind will belong to demons. How can you save others then? The sutras say, 'If you can't cure your own illness, how can you cure others?' Even if you cure your karmic attachment to an illusory body, you still won't leave the demon realm. You will still fear birth and death and won't be able to escape the wheel of existence. Instead, you leave one life for another and take turns wronging each other. The Tathagata appeared in the world to save those who are completely lost and to help them awaken to their own mind. When you chant this mantra, don't give rise to deluded thoughts. This is how you should uphold it."

Names, Terms, and Texts

ALL SANSKRIT WORDS have been romanized without their usual diacritical marks. Also, to approximate actual pronunciation, the ṣ and ś have been written as *sh*, and the ṃ has not been distinguished from *n*. To avoid confusion with other words, I have left *c* unchanged, even though its usual pronunciation approximates English *ch*. I have sometimes used hyphens to clarify the breaks between words, and sometimes I have simply run the words together, as is more common in the romanization of Sanskrit. I continue to find Mainland China's *Pin-yin* romanization system too cruel to use on uninitiated readers and have romanized all Chinese words according to the more traditional and somewhat less bizarre Wade-Giles system, except for place names, in which case I have deleted all apostrophes and dashes, except for the Chinese capital of Ch'ang-an.

Abhidharma 阿毘達磨. Sanskrit for "higher dharmas" or "dharmology," dharmas being the basic building blocks of the mind comparable to the atomic elements of chemistry. Abhidharma also refers to texts that list or discuss such entities.

Abhidharmakosha (bhasaya) 阿毘達磨俱舍論. Considered the quintessential Abhidharma text, this work and its accompanying commentary were composed by Vasubandhu before his conversion to the Mahayana. Its arguments are mainly those of the Sautrantika sect, to which Vasubandhu belonged at the time, and are often critical of Sarvastivadin positions. There exists an English translation by Leo Pruden of de La Valle Poussin's French translation. However, it is not readily available.

Abhisamayalankara Shastra 現觀莊嚴論. Attributed to Asanga, this is one of the most influential commentaries on the Prajnaparamita among Indian and Tibetan Buddhists and is known for its use of both Yogacara and Madhyamaka interpretations. It also supplied the structure used by Conze in organizing his translation of the *Perfection of Wisdom in Twenty-five Thousand Lines.*

Amoghavajra (705–774) 不空. Indian Tantric monk and translator of numerous sutras into Chinese. Although he did not formally translate the *Heart Sutra,* he transcribed the Sanskrit sounds into Chinese, apparently to provide the Chinese with a version that possessed greater spiritual potency. He also included a Chinese translation of individual words. Copies of his transcribed version have been found in the Tunhuang Caves and also among the sutras preserved at Fangshan.

Ananda (b. 432 B.C.) 阿難. Shakyamuni's cousin and attendant, who is said to have repeated the Buddha's sermons from memory at the First Council held in Rajgir several months after the Buddha's Nirvana.

Anathapindada Garden 給孤獨園. Name of the retreat donated to the Buddha by Prince Jeta and the wealthy layman, Sudatta. It was located just outside Shravasti, the capital of the kingdom of Kaushala, and was the scene of many of the Buddha's most important teachings, including the *Diamond Sutra*.

arhan 阿羅漢. The fourth and final stage of practice according to the early followers of the Buddha. It means "worthy of offerings" and was applied to those who had cut off all passions and who were thus free from further rebirth.

Ashoka (d. 232 B.C.) 阿育. Son of Bindusara, whom he succeeded to the throne of the Mauryan dynasty in 268 B.C., and grandson of Candragupta. He is credited with making Buddhism the preeminent religion of the Indian subcontinent. In addition to convening a council of Buddhist elders to ensure the purity of the Order in 267 B.C., he also sent Buddhist missionaries to such border areas as Sri Lanka and Gandhara (Pakistan).

Atthasalini. Ancient oral commentaries (*atthakatha*) edited into written form by Buddhaghosha. There is an English translation under the title *The Expositor* by Pe Maung Tin (London: Pali Text Society, 1976). For the story of the Buddha's ascent to the summit of Mount Sumeru to teach his mother the Abhidharma, see pp. 18–21.

Avalokiteshvara, aka Avalokitasvara 觀自在，觀世音. The interlocutor of the *Heart Sutra* and the most revered of Buddhism's pantheon of bodhisattvas, with thirty-three manifestations, both male and female.

Avatamsaka Sutra 華嚴經. The basic text of the Huayen school of Chinese Buddhism, this "king of sutras" recounts the visits of the youth Sumedha to a series of fifty-three teachers, from whom he learns the teaching of unity and multiplicity. There are two English translations, one by Thomas Cleary and another by the Buddhist Text Translation Society.

Awakening of Faith in the Mahayana 大乘起信論. Exposition of Mahayana philosophy attributed to one of several men named Ashvaghosha who lived in the third century. Some scholars have argued that it was composed in China and not India. Several English translations exist, including those of D. T. Suzuki and Yoshito Hakeda.

Bagchi, S., editor. *The Guhyasamaja Tantra* (Darbhanga, India: The Mithila Institute, 1965).

bhagavan 世尊. One of the ten titles of every buddha. It means "one who bestows prosperity."

Bimbasara 頻婆娑羅. Ruler of the kingdom of Magadha and one of the Buddha's earliest converts. He was later imprisoned and starved to death by his son, Ajatasatru.

Bodhidharma (d. 528) 菩提達磨. Indian monk who introduced Zen to China. I have quoted from my own translation of writings attributed to him: *The Zen Teaching of Bodhidharma* (San Francisco: North Point, 1989). His name also appears as the author of a verse commentary to the *Heart Sutra* written several centuries after his death and preserved in the *Supplement to the Tripitaka*, vol. 113, pp. 942–944.

Bodhiruchi (562–727), aka Dharmaruchi 菩提流志. Not to be confused with an earlier translator of the same name, he was invited to China by Emperor Kao-tsung. Although his translation of the *Heart Sutra* was listed as lost, the *Kaiyuan Index* of A.D. 730 notes: "It was similar to other translations, including Kumarajiva's, and was translated at Foshouchi Temple in 693."

bodhisattva 菩薩. A "spiritual warrior" who resolves to attain enlightenment in order to liberate all beings from suffering and who is thus the paragon of Mahayana Buddhism.

Bodies of Awareness 五蘊. The Five Skandhas.

brahman 婆羅門. A member of India's highest caste. The name was derived from the supreme god of the Vedantins. As hereditary priests, their primary function was the maintenance of ritual order, including the sacred fires.

Buddhadasa (1906–1993). Theravadin monk who urged returning to pristine Buddhism as expressed in early Pali scriptures. Despite his lack of formal education, he was the author of numerous texts and commentaries and helped restore the purity of monastic practice in Thailand. See *Paticcasamuppada: Practical Dependent Origination* (Nonthaburi, Thailand: Vuddhidhamma Fund, 1992).

Buddhaghosha (c. fifth century) 佛鳴. Author of the *Visuddhimagga* (The Path of Purity) and other systematic expositions of Buddhism based on the doctrines of the Sthaviravadin (Theravadin) sect.

Chen-k'o (1543–1603) 真可. Chinese monk known for his knowledge of Taoism and Confucianism as well as Buddhism. He was a close friend of Han-shan Te-ch'ing and is considered one of the four great monks of the Ming dynasty. Among his many accomplishments was the compilation of the Ming dynasty Tripitaka, which he published in 1595. Maligned by his enemies, he died in prison. For a selection of his writings in English, see *Zibo: The Last Great Zen Monk in China* by J. C. Cleary (Berkeley: Asian Humanities Press, 1989). His commentary on the *Heart Sutra* is preserved in the *Supplement to the Tripitaka*, vol. 41, pp. 810–820.

Chia-shan (805–881), aka Shan-hui 夾山. One of the most prominent Zen masters of the late T'ang dynasty, famous for his use of tea as a means of instruction.

Chih-ch'ien (fl. 190–250) 支謙. Born in Loyang to Yueh-chih parents, he became a monk as a young man and studied with Chih-liang, a disciple of Lokakshema. He was later invited to

Nanching by Sun Ch'uan, the king of the state of Wu, and spent over thirty years there translating Buddhist texts before finally retiring to the mountains. Although proponents of the Chinese origin of the *Heart Sutra* dismiss his translation as having never existed, Hui-chiao's *Kaosengchuan* (1), published in 519, lists the *Heart Sutra* (*Prajnaparamita Dharani*) among his translations, as does the *Litai Sanpaochi* (5) of 596.

Chih-hsu (1599–1655) 智旭. One of the four great monks of the Ming dynasty. Although primarily known for his lectures and writings on Tientai Buddhism, he was also interested in Confucianism and even Christianity. His commentary is preserved in the *Supplement to the Tripitaka*, vol. 41, pp. 940–943.

Chih-hui-lun (fl. 840–890), aka Prajnacakra 智慧輪. Indian Tantric monk who served as abbot of Tahsingshan Temple in Ch'ang-an. Although his translation of the longer version of the *Heart Sutra*, dated 861, disappeared in China, a copy was preserved in Japan and has since become part of the current Chinese *Tripitaka*.

Chih-lou-chia-ch'an (fl. 150–190), aka Lokakshema 支婁迦讖. Yueh-chih monk who settled in Loyang and translated some of the first Mahayana scriptures into Chinese, including the *Perfection of Wisdom in Eight Thousand Lines*.

Chih-shen (609–702) 智詵. Student of Hsuan-tsang and also Hung-jen, the Fifth Zen Patriarch. In 696, Empress Wu Tse-t'ien gave Chih-shen the robe transmitted earlier by the Fifth Patriarch to the Sixth Patriarch. Much of Chih-shen's commentary on the *Heart Sutra* incorporates the earlier work of Hui-ching. His commentary was originally lost, but several copies were found in the Tunhuang Caves. I have used the collated edition published by Fang K'uang-ch'ang, *Po-jo hsin-ching yi-chu chi-ch'eng*, pp. 239–265.

Ching-chueh (683–750) 淨覺. Disciple of Shen-hsiu and Hsuan-che, both of whom were disciples of Hung-jen, the Fifth Patriarch of Zen, and both of whom were considered founders of China's Northern School of Zen. Ching-chueh was the author of one of the earliest accounts of the Northern School, an English translation of which appears in *Zen Dawn* by J. C. Cleary (Boston: Shambhala, 1986). Although his commentary, dated 727, disappeared soon after it was written, several copies were found in the Tunhuang Caves. I have used the collated edition published by Fang K'uang-ch'ang, ibid., pp. 336–361.

Ching-mai (fl. 650) 靖邁. Chinese monk who served for a number of years as a member of Hsuan-tsang's translation staff. His commentary, which reflects the Yogacara views of his teacher, is preserved in the *Supplement to the Tripitaka*, vol. 41, pp. 425–435.

Chuang-tzu (369–286 B.C.) 莊子. Ranked after Lao-tzu in the Taoist pantheon of sages, he was the author of the collection of Taoist fables and allegories that bears his name. His book has been translated into English many times, including by Burton Watson.

Conze, Edward (1904–1979). Western scholar of Buddhism who devoted most of his academic career to the study and elucidation of Prajnaparamita texts. His translation of the *Perfection of Wisdom in Twenty-five Thousand Lines* is available as *The Large Sutra of Perfect Wisdom* (Berkeley: University of California Press, 1975). His editions and translations of the *Heart Sutra* are contained in his *Buddhist Wisdom Books* (London: Allen and Unwin, 1958) and *Thirty Years of Buddhist Studies* (Oxford: Bruno Cassirer, 1967). His discussion of Prajnaparamita texts can be found in *The Prajnaparamita Literature* (New Delhi: Munshiram Manoharlal, 2000).

Cox, Collett. "On the Possibility of a Nonexistent Object of Consciousness: Sarvastivadin and Darshtantika Theories" in the *Journal of the International Association of Buddhist Studies*, vol. 11, no. 1, 1988.

Deva (fl. 250), aka Aryadeva 提婆. Student of Nagarjuna and author of several seminal works that helped lay the foundation of the Madhyamaka interpretation of the Dharma. The *Heart Sutra* commentary attributed to him is preserved in the *Supplement to the Tripitaka*, vol. 41, pp. 629–634.

devas 天. One of six major categories of being. Devas represent the more fortunate karmic outcome of delusion and inhabit the various heavens on Mount Sumeru, where they live long and blissful lives until the karma that got them there runs out. They are, however, capable of understanding the Dharma and are often present in the Buddha's audience in Mahayana sutras.

dharani 陀羅尼. An incantation with mnemonic value as well as spiritual potency. Also see *mantra*.

dharma 法. Derived from the root *dhri*, meaning "to grasp," this word refers to anything held to be real: an object, an event, a teaching, a code. For students of the Abhidharma, it referred to such basic entities of the mind as the Five Skandhas. When capitalized, it refers to the teaching of a buddha.

dharma-kaya 法身. The real body of every buddha and synonymous with reality.

Dharmaskandha 法蘊足論. A selection of the Buddha's sermons in Shravasti focusing on the dharmas that later formed the *matrika* (matrices) of the Abhidharma. This is considered the first or second of the seven canonical Abhidharma works of the Sarvastivadins and is given a date of c. 300 B.C. While the Chinese attribute this work to Maudgalyayana, Yashomitra ascribes it to Shariputra. A number of commentators have noted its similarity to the *Vibhanga* of the Sthaviravadins, and both texts probably share a common ancestor.

Dhirgha Agama 長阿含經. One of four collections of the Buddha's sermons preserved in Sanskrit by the Sarvastivadins. The only extant version is a Chinese translation by Buddhayashas. It is similar but not identical to the Pali *Digha Nikaya* of the Sthaviravadins.

Diamond Sutra, *Vajracchedika* 金剛經. Next to the *Heart Sutra*, the best known of all Prajnaparamita texts and the subject of many studies and commentaries. Its central teaching is the nature of a buddha's body. There are numerous translations and also several commentaries in English.

Eighteen Elements of Perception, *ashtadasha dhatu* 十八界. The explanation of our awareness as a combination of the Six Powers and the Six Domains of Sensation and the Six Kinds of Consciousness that arise from their conjunction.

Fa-ch'eng (fl. 840), aka Chos-grub 法成. Tibetan monk who lived in Tunhuang and translated a number of Buddhist works from Chinese into Tibetan. He also translated the longer version of the *Heart Sutra* from Tibetan into Chinese. His translation, however, was not added to the Chinese Tripitaka until a copy turned up in the Tunhuang Caves (P4882).

Fa-tsang (643–712) 法藏. Born in Ch'ang-an of Sogdian parents from Samarkand, he learned Sanskrit and a number of Central Asian languages at an early age. Not long after becoming a monk, he was invited to participate in the translation projects of Hsuan-tsang and Yi-ching. But he is better known for his own essays and commentaries and as the principal patriarch of the Hua-yen (Avatamsaka) school of Chinese Buddhism. His *Heart Sutra* commentary, composed in 702, became so popular that it was, itself, the object of commentaries. His commentary, along with a subcommentary by Chung-hsi, is preserved in the *Supplement to the Tripitaka*, vol. 41, pp. 679–712.

Fa-yueh (653–743), aka Dharmacandra 法月. Monk from Eastern India who arrived in Ch'ang-an in 732 via Kucha. Although primarily interested in medical texts, he is credited with the first Chinese translation of the longer version of the *Heart Sutra*, which he is said to have brought with him from Kucha. Before leaving Ch'ang-an in 741, he also produced a second, revised translation of the longer version. The revised translation is in the Chinese Tripitaka, while his initial version is preserved in the Japanese Tripitaka (cf. Fang Ku'ang-ch'ang, ibid., pp. 5–6).

Fang K'uang-ch'ang 方廣錩. Chinese Buddhist scholar. His collection and review of Chinese translations of the *Heart Sutra* and early commentaries, several of which he has revised on the basis of Tunhuang copies, is invaluable: *Po-jo hsin-ching yi-chu chi-ch'eng* (Shanghai: Shanghai Kuchi Publishing Company, 1994).

Five Skandhas, *panca skandha* 五蘊. The aspects into which early Buddhists analyzed our experiential world—form, sensation, perception, memory, and consciousness—and which formed the basis for the subsequent development of the Abhidharma.

Four Elements 四大. The division of the material world into earth, water, wind, and fire.

Four Teachings 四教. Chinese monks used several schemes for
classifying the Buddha's teachings according to his audience.
The one used by Ming-k'uang agrees with that of the Tientai
patriarch Chih-yi (538–597) and includes the Hinayana Teaching
for shravakas, the Common Teaching for pratyekas, the Special
Teaching for beginning bodhisattvas, and the Complete Teaching for fully realized bodhisattvas.

Four (Noble) Truths, *catvari (arya) satyani* 四（聖）諦. A frequent
subject of the Buddha's teaching and also the subject of his first
sermon at Sarnath: suffering, the origin of suffering, the cessation of suffering, and the path leading to the cessation of suffering: *duhkha, samudaya, nirodha, marga.*

Frauwallner, Erich. *Studies in Abhidharma Literature and the Origins
of Buddhist Philosophical Systems* (Albany: State University of New
York Press, 1995).

Fukui, Fumimasa. *Hannya shingyo no kenkyu* (Tokyo: Shunjusha,
1987).

Heart Sutra, (Prajnaparamita) Hridaya Sutra （般若波羅蜜多）
心經. This briefest of texts contrasts the teaching of Prajnaparamita with the Abhidharma of the Sarvastivadins and presents, in place of their standard conceptual matrix, a mantra as
the essence of its teaching. This sutra was translated from Sanskrit into Chinese in two versions, an earlier, shorter version and

a later, longer one. There are many translations and also commentaries in English.

Hinayana 小乘. The Lesser Path of Buddhism. A term coined by the Mahayana to distinguish its compassion-based practices from sects or individuals whose ascetic practices aimed at personal salvation and nirvana.

Hsuan-tsang (602–664) 玄奘. China's most famous Buddhist monk. Although better known for his journey to India and back, he was one of the most prolific translators of Buddhist scriptures into Chinese. Despite their faithfulness to the letter of his texts, his translations are also noted for their awkward phraseology. The fact that his version of the *Heart Sutra* is one of the most chanted texts in the Buddhist liturgy is apparently the result of his use of Kumarajiva's earlier version.

Huai-shen (1077–1132) 懷深, aka Tz'u-shou. Zen monk of the Yunmen sect. His commentary appears in the *Supplement to the Tripitaka*, vol. 41, pp. 781–792.

Hui-ching (578–650) 慧淨. Chinese monk known for his literary and lecturing abilities. Asked by Emperor T'ai-tsung to help Hsuan-tsang translate the sutras he had brought back from India, Hui-ching declined on the pretext of illness. His commentary, which was among the most influential during the T'ang dynasty, appears in the *Supplement to the Tripitaka*, vol. 41, pp. 411–424. For the most part, I have used the revised edition of Fang K'uang-ch'ang based on a comparison of the Tripitaka edition with copies found in the Tunhuang Caves.

Hui-chung (d. 775) 慧忠. Although he was considered one of the five dharma heirs of Hui-neng, the Sixth Patriarch of Zen, Hui-chung was critical of other members of the Southern School of Zen, such as Ma-tsu, for their disdain of scriptures and offhand interpretations of the Dharma. He was the teacher of a series of emperors and was given the appellation Teacher of the Nation by Emperor Hsuan-tsung. His commentary, which reflects the radical attitude toward enlightenment of the early Zen school, is preserved, together with those of two Sung dynasty monks, in the *Supplement to the Tripitaka*, vol. 41, pp. 781–792.

Hui-neng (638–713) 慧能. Zen's Sixth Patriarch and founder of its Southern School.

Hung-jen (602–675) 弘忍. Fifth Patriarch of Zen and teacher of Hui-neng, Shen-hsiu, Chih-shen, and Ching-chueh. The use of the *Diamond Sutra* in place of the *Lankavatara Sutra* in teaching the principles of Zen is said to have begun with him.

Indra, aka Shakra 天帝. King of the Devas. His residence is at the summit of Mount Sumeru. He serves as a major figure in Prajnaparamita texts and frequently asks questions of the Buddha or his disciples.

Jain 耆那. Member of the religion begun in India by Mahavira in the fifth century B.C. emphasizing non-violence and liberation of the soul.

Jnanamitra. Indian author of a commentary on the *Heart Sutra* about whom next to nothing is known. His exposition was translated into English by Donald Lopez in *Elaborations on Emptiness* (Princeton, N.J.: Princeton University Press, 1996, pp. 141–150).

kalpa 劫. A period of time from the creation to the destruction of the universe. An empty kalpa is the period of time between universes.

Kanishka (fl. A.D. 100–125) 迦膩色迦. The greatest of the Kushan kings and advocate of religious diversity. His support of Buddhism can be seen in his use of the images of Shakyamuni and Maitreya on his coins and in the many Buddhist legends surrounding his reign. According to the inscription on his stupa, he was a supporter of the Sarvastivadin sect and is credited with convening a major Buddhist council, often called the Fourth Council.

Katyayaniputra (fl. 270 B.C.) 迦多衍尼子. One of the leaders of the Sarvastivadin delegation at the Third Buddhist Council held in Pataliputra (Patna) in 267 B.C. To clarify the Sarvastivadin position vis-à-vis the Sthaviravadins, he later compiled the *Jnanaprasthana* (Source of Knowledge), which became the most studied of all Sarvastivadin Abhidharma texts. There are two Chinese translations, but the text is no longer extant in Sanskrit, except for fragments.

Kinsley, David. *Tantric Visions of the Divine Feminine: The Ten Mahavidyas* (Berkeley: University of California Press, 1997).

K'uei-chi (632–682), aka Tz'u-en 窺基. The best known of Hsuan-tsang's disciples, he wrote commentaries on many of the Yogacara texts translated by his teacher. He also wrote commentaries on the scriptures of other sects, but from a Yogacara viewpoint. In the case of the *Heart Sutra*, however, he commented from both the Yogacara and the Madhyamaka perspectives. His commentary has been translated into English in its entirety by Heng-ching as part of the BDK translation series. The Chinese is preserved in the *Supplement to the Tripitaka*, vol. 41, pp. 436–478.

Kumarajiva (d. 413) 鳩摩羅什. A renowned monk from the Silk Road oasis of Kucha. Originally a follower of the Sarvastivadin sect, he was converted to the Mahayana while in India and came to China at the request of the reigning emperor. Generally considered the greatest translator of Buddhist scriptures into Chinese, he often took advantage of the earlier work of other translators and focused on the spirit rather than the letter of his texts.

Kushan Empire. Established by the nomadic Yueh-chih in the regions north and south of the Hindu Kush Mountains during the first century B.C. It formed the backdrop, if not the seedbed, for the development and spread of Mahayana Buddhism.

Lankavatara Sutra 楞伽經 . This sutra was translated at least three times into Chinese and was reportedly used by Bodhidharma and others in the early transmission of Zen in China. This is an early product of the Yogacara school of Indian Buddhism and presents that school's Mind-Only doctrine in the form of a dialogue between the Buddha and the bodhisattva Mahamati. There is an English translation by D. T. Suzuki.

Lao-tzu (c. 604–516 B.C.) 老子. Taoist patriarch and author of the *Taoteching,* probably the most translated book in the world next to the Bible and the *Bhagavad-gita.*

Leonard, George. *The Silent Pulse* (New York: Bantam Books, 1981).

Lesser Path, aka Hinayana Buddhism 小乘. A term coined by Mahayana Buddhists to refer to those who focused on the personal attainment of nirvana in contrast to the liberation of all beings.

Li-yen (c. 710–795) 利言. Buddhist monk from the Silk Road oasis of Kucha who assisted Fa-yueh and Prajna in their translations of the longer version of the *Heart Sutra* in Ch'ang-an.

Longer Sukhavativyuha Sutra 無量壽經. This is one of three texts that form the basis of Pure Land Buddhism. It records the vows of the bodhisattva Dharmakara to create a pure land that can be reached by faith alone and from which one can then more easily understand the Dharma. The text is still extant in Sanskrit, and there are translations in Chinese, Tibetan, and English.

Lopez, Donald. *Elaborations on Emptiness: Uses of the Heart Sutra* (Princeton, N. J.: Princeton University Press, 1996). See also his earlier effort: *The Heart Sutra Explained: Indian and Tibetan Commentaries* (Albany: State University of New York Press, 1988).

Lotus Sutra (妙法) 蓮華經. One of the earliest Mahayana texts and especially revered by China's Tientai and Japan's Nichiren sects. In addition to presenting the cosmic aspects of the Buddha, it encourages all beings to realize their own buddha-nature. There are a number of English translations.

Madhyamaka 中觀派 . The Middle Way school of Indian Buddhism founded by Nagarjuna and based on the Prajnaparamita teaching of emptiness.

Madhyamakakarika 中論. One of the seminal texts of the Madhyamaka school of Indian Buddhism. Written by Nagarjuna, it presents the Madhyamaka position concerning causality as well as existence and non-existence. There are a number of English translations, ranging from the scholarly, by David Kalupahana, to the more literary, by Stephen Batchelor.

Maha Prajnaparamita Shastra 大智度論. Nagarjuna's magnum opus, this is a commentary on the *Perfection of Wisdom in Twenty-five Thousand Lines.* There is a French translation by Etienne Lamotte under the title *Le Trait de la Grande Vertu de Sagesse.*

Maha Prajnaparamita Sutra 大般若波羅蜜多經. This is an encyclopedic collection of Prajnaparamita scriptures. It was translated into Chinese by Hsuan-tsang and his staff from 660 to 663.

Mahavastu 大事. Account of the Buddha's life compiled by the Mahasanghikas, one of two sects that formed as a result of differences at Buddhism's Second Council in 283 B.C.

Mahavibhasha Shastra 大毘婆沙論. A collection of commentaries on Katyayaniputra's *Jnanaprasthana* compiled by dozens, if not hundreds, of monks in Kashmir around A.D. 100–150. It is only extant in Chinese.

Mahavira 摩訶毘羅. Founder of the Jain religion. He was a contemporary of Shakyamuni and taught the purification of the soul through non-violence as the principal means for attaining nirvana. Depending on whose dating one accepts for the Buddha, Mahavira entered Nirvana either around 490 B.C. or 390 B.C., or about seven years before the Buddha.

Mahayana 大乘. The Great Path or Great Vehicle, depending on the meaning one gives *yana.* This teaching aims at the liberation of all beings. It is also another name for the mind.

Mair, Victor. "The Heart Sutra and The Journey to the West" in *Sino-Asiatica: Papers Dedicated to Professor Liu Ts'un-yan on the Occasion of His 85th Birthday* (Wang Gungwu et al., editors, Canberra: Faculty of Asian Studies of the Australian National University, 2002).

Maitreya 彌勒. The next buddha after Shakyamuni. Usually portrayed by Buddhists in East Asia as a rotund, smiling monk, his statue is often the first to greet visitors as they enter a Buddhist temple in East Asia.

mantra 咒. An incantation with spiritual potency composed of sounds that do not necessarily make sense.

Maudgalyayana 目犍連. The childhood companion of Shariputra and one of the Buddha's foremost disciples. He was known for his supernatural powers and is usually represented in art as standing on the Buddha's left.

Maya 摩耶. The wife of Shuddhodana and mother of the Buddha. She died seven days after giving birth to Shakyamuni and was reborn as the deva Santushita at the summit of Mount Sumeru.

Ming-k'uang (fl. 650) 明曠. Disciple of the Tientai patriarch Chang-an. His commentary, which interprets the *Heart Sutra* according to the Tientai doctrine of four levels of teaching (Hinayana, Common, Special, Complete), disappeared in China but made its way to Japan. It is preserved in the *Supplement to the Tripitaka*, vol. 41, pp. 656–659.

Monier-Williams, Monier (1819–1899). British Sanskrit scholar whose *Sanskrit–English Dictionary*, published in 1872 and based on the monumental *Sanskrit–Deutsch Woerterbuch* of Boehtlingk and Roth, remains the standard reference. It is available in reprint editions and online.

Mount Sumeru 須彌山. This mountain forms the axis of every world and is often used as a metaphor for the self. According to Buddhist cosmology, the summit is the second of six heavens in the Realm of Desire (the first heaven being halfway up the mountain, and the other four being above the summit). This is also the home of thirty-three devas, including Indra, their king, and Santushita, the former mother of Shakyamuni.

Nagarjuna (fl. A.D. 175–200) 龍樹. The founder of the Madhyamaka school of Indian Buddhism and author of several seminal texts that refute standpoints advocating existence or non-existence. In their place, he advocated *shunyata*, or emptiness, as the true nature of things. Thus, the *Heart Sutra* is often seen as deriving from Nagarjuna or his disciples or possibly even his teachers.

Nakamura, Hajime (1912–present). The doyen among Japanese scholars specializing in Indian Buddhism. For his works in English, see his *Indian Buddhism* (Tokyo: Sanseido Press, 1980) and *Gotama Buddha* (Rutland, Vt.: Tuttle, 2001).

Nattier, Jan. "The *Heart Sutra*: A Chinese Apocryphal Text?" in *The Journal of the International Association of Buddhist Studies*, 1992, pp. 153–223; *A Few Good Men: The Bodhisattva Path According to the Inquiry of Ugra* (Honolulu: University of Hawaii Press, 2003).

nirmana-kaya 化身. The body manifested by a buddha for use in teaching others. However, this body is still subject to karma and is not a buddha's real body, or *dharma-kaya*.

nirvana 涅槃. Interpreted as referring to a flame (namely, the flame of passion) that has been blown out, this was the word used to describe the goal of early Buddhists. It was used as an equivalent for liberation but also for death followed by no further rebirth. Thus, it was the focus of such sects as the Sarvastivadins but was replaced by enlightenment among later Mahayana Buddhists, whose goal was to stay in the world and help others.

Nyaya Sutras 尼夜耶經. A series of early works on logic (*nyaya* means "sound argument") attributed to Gautama Akshapada (c. second century A.D.) and on the basis of which a school of philosophy of the same name developed. Several English translations are available.

Padoux, Andre. In *Understanding Mantras* (Harvey Alper, editor, Albany: State University of New York Press, 1989).

Pao-t'ung (732–824) 寶通. Student of Shih-t'ou (700–790), the patriarch of Japan's Soto Zen sect, and a close friend of Han Yu, the greatest Confucian figure of the T'ang dynasty. The stupa containing Pao-t'ung's tongue still stands at Lingshan Temple south of Chaochou in Kuangtung province. His commentary on the *Heart Sutra* is preserved in the *Supplement to the Tripitaka*, vol. 42, pp. 67–70.

Patisambhidamagga 無礙解道. One of the earliest Abhidharma texts in the Pali Canon, it is attributed to Shariputra. However, its initial composition probably took place a hundred years later in the third century B.C. It was later incorporated into the *Khuddaka Nikaya*. There is an English translation available from the Pali Text Society, and it also exists in Chinese.

Perfection of Wisdom in Eight Thousand Lines, Ashtasahasrika Prajnaparamita Sutra 小品般若波羅蜜經. Considered the earliest of the Prajnaparamita sutras. Chinese translations include those by Lokakshema in A.D. 180, Kumarajiva in A.D. 382, and Hsuan-tsang in A.D. 660. There are several English translations: *The Perfection of Wisdom in Eight Thousand Lines & Its Verse Summary* by Edward Conze (San Francisco: Four Seasons Foundation, 1973) and *Mother of the Buddhas* by Lex Hixon (Wheaton, Ill.: Quest Books, 1993).

Perfection of Wisdom in One Hundred Thousand Lines, Shatasahasrika Prajnaparamita 大般若波羅蜜多經. This is the longest of all Prajnaparamita texts. It is extant in Sanskrit as well as in Chinese and Tibetan, and is the first of the sixteen sutras that make up the *Maha Prajnaparamita Sutra.*

Perfection of Wisdom in Twenty-five Thousand Lines, Pancavimshati-sahasrika Prajnaparamita Sutra 摩訶般若波羅蜜經. One of the most comprehensive treatments of the teaching of Prajnaparamita. This text was translated into Chinese on four occasions: by Dharmaraksha in A.D. 286, by Mokshala in A.D. 291, by Kumarajiva in A.D. 404, and by Hsuan-tsang in A.D. 663. For an English translation from the Sanskrit, see *The Large Sutra on Perfect Wisdom* by Edward Conze (Berkeley: University of California Press, 1975).

Potter, Karl, editor. *Encyclopedia of Indian Philosophies* (New Delhi: Motilal Banarsidass, 1996, vol. 7).

Prajna (fl. 790) 般若. Indian monk who translated the longer version of the *Heart Sutra* together with Li-yen in 790. This is also the word for "wisdom" or "insight" and is the focus, along with compassion, of Mahayana practice.

Prajnaparamita 般若波羅蜜多. This is the name of the teaching that formed the basis of Mahayana Buddhism. It is also the name of the goddess who embodies the teaching, and thus reality. The Sanskrit means "transcendent wisdom" or "perfection of wisdom," depending on how one parses the word *paramita.*

pratyeka-buddha 緣覺. A religious practitioner who achieves enlightenment by and for himself.

Pravaradevaraja Paripriccha Sutra 勝天王般若波羅. Translated into Chinese in 565 by Upashunya and a hundred years later by Hsuan-tsang as part of his *Maha Prajnaparamita Sutra*, this sutra records the Buddha's exposition of the meaning and practice of Prajnaparamita in answer to the questions of the deva Pravara.

Pure Land 淨土宗. Buddhist sect that encourages practitioners to put their faith in Amitabha Buddha, who has created a paradise where they will be reborn if they will only invoke that buddha's name. And once reborn in his paradise, they will more easily understand the Dharma and achieve liberation.

Purnaprabhasa Samadhimati Sutra 成具光明定意經. Translated into Chinese by Chih-yao in A.D. 185.

Rajgir 王舍城. Capital of the kingdom of Magadha in Northeast India and the scene of many of the Buddha's sermons.

Ratnagunasancaya Gatha 佛母寶德藏般若波羅蜜經. One of the earliest known examples of the Prajnaparamita teaching, usually given a date of c. 100 B.C.

Realm of Desire 欲界. The lowest of the Three Realms (Triloka) of existence (psychic or otherwise), the other two being the Realms of Form and Formlessness far above Mount

Sumeru. Existence in the Realm of Desire is dominated by desire for food, sex, and sleep. At its base this realm is the home of sinners, hungry ghosts, animals, and humans. Above this is a series of six heavens. The first heaven, halfway up Mount Sumeru, is occupied by asuras and the Four Guardians. The second heaven is the Trayatrinsha Heaven, the abode of Indra and thirty-two other devas, at the summit of Mount Sumeru. And the remaining four heavens above Mount Sumeru are the abode of Yama (Judge of the Dead), the abode of future buddhas (Tushita), the abode of those born in bliss (Nirmanarati), and the abode of Shiva and Mara (Paranirmita-vashavarin).

Red Pine 赤松. *The Zen Teaching of Bodhidharma* (Berkeley: North Point Press, 1987); *Lao-tzu's Taoteching* (San Francisco: Mercury House Press, 1996); *The Diamond Sutra* (Washington, D.C.: Counterpoint Press, 2001).

samadhi 三昧. The state in which the mind is focused on one, or even no, object.

Samyukt Agama 雜阿含經. One of several sutra collections of the Sarvastivadins containing the early teachings of the Buddha. Similar, but not identical, to the *Samyutta Nikaya* of the Sthaviravadins (Theravadins), it only exists in Chinese, into which it was translated by the Indian monk Gunabhadra between the years 435 and 445 in Nanching. Gunabhadra also translated the *Lankavatara Sutra* and was considered by some to be the First Patriarch of Zen in China.

sanbhoga-kaya 報身. The body that is created by every bodhisattva and buddha upon vowing to liberate all beings. Such a body, however, is not fully realized until enlightenment. As with the *nirmana-kaya*, it, too, is still subject to karma and is not a buddha's real body.

Sangitiparyaya 眾集經. A commentary on the *Sangiti Sutra*, which is the ninth of the thirty sutras that make up the *Dhirgha Agama*. The Chinese attribute this expository work to Shariputra, while Yashomitra and Bu-ston ascribe it to Kaushthila. Organized around numerical lists of dharmas, this was probably the earliest known attempt at a systematic presentation of the Sarvastivadin Abhidharma. The only extant version is a Chinese translation by Hsuan-tsang.

Sankasya 僧伽施. Location in India where the Buddha descended to earth following his summer-long sojourn in the Trayatrinsha Heaven teaching his mother the Abhidharma. One of King Ashoka's pillars marks the spot not far from Pakhra on the train line that runs through modern Farrukhabad.

sansara 生死. Life and death, the place where all suffering takes place. The paramitas, or perfections, are often viewed as taking us from this shore of sansara to the other shore of nirvana.

Santushita 知足. After her death, the Buddha's mother was reborn as this deva in the Trayatrinsha Heaven at the summit of Mount Sumeru. The name means "perfect bliss."

Sarvastivada 一切有部. The teaching that "all entities are real." This was also the name of one of the most prominent and wide-spread early Buddhist sects in Northern and Central India as well as Central Asia. It is this teaching with which the first half of the *Heart Sutra* is contrasted. Unfortunately, much of our knowledge of this sect is based on texts, such as Vasubandhu's *Abhidharmakosha*, that are critical of it. Although there is very little in English on this sect or its teaching, for a useful survey of the literature see *Sarvastivada Buddhist Scholasticism* by Charles Willemen, Bart Dessein, and Collett Cox (Leiden: Brill, 1998), as well as the works by Frauwallner and Potter cited earlier.

Sautrantikas 經量部. Buddhist sect that developed from the Darshtantikas. As their name suggests, they only accepted the sutras as the authentic teaching of the Dharma.

Seng-chao (384–414) 僧肇. The most prominent disciple of Kumarajiva and the author of a set of philosophical works known collectively as the *Chaolun*, which has been translated into English by Walter Liebenthal and others.

Shakyamuni 釋迦牟尼. The "sage of the Shakyas," the Shakyas being the clan into which the Buddha was born.

Shariputra 舍利子. The "son of Shari" and companion of Maudgalyayana, he was considered the wisest of the Buddha's disciples and the author of the earliest texts on the Abhidharma, which is why he appears in this sutra.

shastra 論. Exposition of Buddhist doctrine by later followers of the Buddha.

Shen-hsiu (605–706) 神秀. Although he was the foremost disciple of Hung-jen, the Fifth Zen Patriarch, later Zen tradition traced the patriarchship through Hui-neng, who became leader of the Southern School of Zen, while Shen-hsiu was viewed as leader of the Northern School.

Shih-hu (fl. 985), aka Danapala 施護. Monk from the Northern Indian kingdom of Udyana (Swat). He arrived in the Sung dynasty capital of Kaifeng in 980 together with the Indian monk T'ien-hsi-tsai (d. 1000) and worked on translations of mostly Tantric texts at Kuohsing Temple. His translation of the *Heart Sutra* was that of the longer version.

Shikshananda (652–710) 實叉難陀. Khotanese monk who worked on translations of the *Avatamsaka* and *Lankavatara* sutras between 695 and 705 at Foshouchi Temple in Loyang. In the *Kaiyuan Index* of 730, his translation of the *Heart Sutra* was already listed as missing.

shravaka 聲聞. Sanskrit term meaning "hearer," it originally referred to the immediate disciples of the Buddha who "heard" him speak. Later, it was used to refer to any follower of the sects denigrated by the Mahayana as Hinayana and used in contrast to the bodhisattva. Thus, the goal of shravakas is nirvana and not enlightenment.

Shravasti 舍衛. The capital of the kingdom of Kaushala and the largest city in India during the Buddha's day. This is where the Buddha spent many of his monsoon seasons, and it was from here that he ascended to the summit of Mount Sumeru, where he taught his mother the Abhidharma during the seventh monsoon following his Enlightenment.

shunyata 空. Sanskrit for "emptiness." The meaning is not "space" but just the opposite: the absence of the falsely conceived space between entities of the mind or those of the material world created by discrimination.

Six Perfections, *sad paramita* 六度. The practices that guide a bodhisattva's quest for enlightenment: generosity (*dana* 布施), morality (*shila* 持戒), forbearance (*kshanti* 忍辱), vigor (*virya* 精進), meditation (*dhyana* 闡定), and wisdom (*prajna* 智慧).

Sixth Patriarch 六祖. See Hui-neng.

skandhas 蘊. See Five Skandhas.

srota-apanna 須陀洹. The first of the four stages on the shravaka path that leads to nirvana. It means "to find the river," the river of impermanence.

Sthaviravadins 上座部. One of the two major Buddhist sects that formed during the century following the Buddha's Nirvana in 383 B.C. The other sect was the Mahasanghikas. The Sthaviravadins subsequently split into a dozen sects, among which were the Sarvastivadins. The Theravadin sect of Sri Lanka and Southeast Asia also traces its ancestry to the Sthaviravadins.

Sumeru 須彌. The mountain that forms the axis of every world and that is often used as a metaphor for the self. See Mount Sumeru.

Supplement to the Tripitaka 續藏經. Monumental compilation of Chinese Buddhist works by Japanese Buddhists completed in Kyoto in 1915. It includes a number of texts lost in China but preserved in Japan. The edition I have used was published in Taipei in 1994 by Hsinwenfeng in a set of 150 volumes. I have quoted mostly from volume 41, which contains 36 commentaries on the *Heart Sutra*.

sutra 經. A sermon attributed to the Buddha, one of his immediate disciples, or someone empowered by a buddha to speak on his or her behalf.

Suzuki, Shunryu (1904–1971). Japanese monk who arrived in America in 1959 and established Soto Zen practice in the San Francisco area. His teachings have been edited into a number of volumes, the best known of which is *Zen Mind, Beginner's Mind* (Tokyo: Weatherhill, 1970). See also *Not Always So* (New York: HarperCollins, 2002).

Tao-lung (1213–1278) 道隆. Buddhist monk noted for his work in transmitting Zen to Japan.

tathagata 如來. One of every buddha's ten titles. It can mean "one who has gone thus" or "one who has come thus," "thus" referring to that state that is ineffable and beyond language.

Te-ch'ing (1546–1623), aka Han-shan (憨山)德清. One of the four great Buddhist monks of the Ming dynasty and instrumental in reviving the practice of Zen in China. His voluminous writings include commentaries on Confucian and Taoist works as well as Buddhist texts. His *Heart Sutra* commentary is preserved in the *Supplement to the Tripitaka,* vol. 41, pp. 842–847.

Testament Sutra 遺教經. Translated into Chinese by Kumarajiva, this text relates the Buddha's final instructions before entering Nirvana. There is also a commentary by Vasubandhu extant in Chinese.

Three Insights, *tri-vidya* 三明. The insights into the essential characteristics of all dharmas: impermanence, suffering, and no self.

Three Realms 三界. See Realm of Desire.

Trayatrinsha 忉利天. The name of the second of the six heavens in the Realm of Desire. This heaven is located at the very summit of Mount Sumeru and is the residence of Indra, King of the Devas. It was also where the Buddha taught the deva San-tushita the Abhidharma.

Tripitaka 三藏 . The Buddhist Canon of received scriptures. Although many Sanskrit texts still exist, the largest collections are in Chinese, Pali, and Tibetan.

Tunhuang Caves, aka Mokao Caves 敦煌石窟. Series of shrines carved into a hillside outside the Silk Road oasis of Tunhuang in Northwest China. Thousands of manuscripts sealed in a side cave were discovered by a Taoist priest at the turn of the last century and sold to foreign collectors such as Aurel Stein (S) and Paul Pelliot (P), whose copies are preserved in their respective national archives in London and Paris. A number of copies also made their way to libraries and private collections in Japan and America as well as Beijing.

Twelve Abodes of Sensation, *dvadashanga ayatana* 十二處. The Six Powers of Sensation: eyes, ears, nose, tongue, body, and mind, along with the Six Domains of Sensation: color and shape, sound, smell, taste, feeling, and thought. An early formula used in meditation to view our experience as a set of transitory, inter-dependent elements.

Twelve Links of Dependent Origination, *dvadashanga pratitya-samutpada*, aka *dvadashanga nidana* 十二緣起. Ignorance, memory, consciousness, name and form, six senses, contact, sensation, thirst, attachment, existence, birth, old age and death. A formula used in meditation to understand the nature of our experience by viewing it as a series of interdependent states dependent on other states and thus without a permanent, independent self.

Two Paths/Vehicles 二乘. Another reference to the Hinayana Path, which it divides into the path of the shravakas and the path of the pratyeka-buddhas.

Vasubandhu (316–396) 世親. Indian monk and younger brother of Asanga. He was the author of the *Abhidharmakosha* as well as the *Abhidharmakoshabhasaya*, which was a commentary on the former. Together these two works present the Sarvastivadin view of the Abhidharma, though from the standpoint of the Sautrantika sect. Apparently, Vasubandhu belonged to the Sarvastivadin and Sautrantika sects before his brother convinced him of the superiority of the Mahayana.

Vibhanga 毘崩伽. Early Pali work similar to the Sanskrit *Dharmaskandha* of the Sarvastivadins and among the earliest attempts to enumerate the dharmas of the Abhidharma.

Vimalakirti Sutra 維摩詰經. One of the most popular Mahayana sutras, it features the visit by Manjushri to the sick layman Vimalakirti, who serves as an example of the high level of attainment possible outside a monastic environment. Several Chinese and Tibetan translations are extant, and there are also a number in English.

vinaya 律. That part of the Buddhist Tripitaka that contains the texts listing the rules that govern the lives of Buddhist monastic and lay followers.

Watanabe, Shogo. "A Comparative Study of the *Pancavinshatisa-hasrika Prajnaparamita*" in the *Journal of the American Oriental Society*, 1994.

Yi-ching (635–713) 義淨. Chinese monk who traveled to India in 671 and translated a number of sutras and vinaya texts after his return in 695. His translation of the *Heart Sutra* was made in 706 at Chienfu Temple in Ch'ang-an but was lost in China. A copy later turned up in Japan, but scholars remain divided over its authenticity.

Yin-shun (1906–present) 印順. One of the foremost Chinese scholars of early Indian Buddhism and the Madhyamaka philosophy of Nagarjuna. His *Heart Sutra* commentary was delivered in 1947 as a series of talks at Hsuehtou Temple in Chekiang province following the death of his teacher, Master T'ai-hsu (1889–1947). It can be found in his *Po-jo-ching chiang-chi* (Taipei: Cheng-wen, 1998).

Yogacara 瑜伽行. This term means the "practice of yoga," but in its application in Buddhism it refers to the school of Mahayana that viewed the world and its objects as made of mind alone and that consequently engaged in a detailed analysis of consciousness as the means for liberation.

Yuan-tse (613–696), aka Wonchuk 圓測. Korean disciple of Hsuan-tsang known for his commentaries on his teacher's translations. His commentary on the *Heart Sutra* is preserved in the *Supplement to the Tripitaka*, vol. 41, pp. 635–655.

Yueh-chih, aka Tokharians, Kushans 月支. Nomadic tribe inhabiting the pastures of the Chilien Mountains south of the Silk Road oasis of Tunhuang, where they are recorded as living as early as 1000 B.C. Following a series of defeats by the nomadic Hsiung-nu in the second century B.C., one branch of the Yueh-chih migrated westward and eventually established the Kushan Empire with its center in what are now Uzbekistan, Afghanistan, and Pakistan.

The *Heart Sutra*

The Longer Version

I N ADDITION to the standard text of the *Heart Sutra* that forms the basis of this book, there is a longer version. This longer version appeared in China as early as the eighth century and was translated into Chinese at least six times: by Fa-yueh (Dharmacandra) around 735 and again around 740, by Prajna and Li-yen in 790, by Fa-ch'eng (Chos-grub) from the Tibetan around 845, by Chih-hui-lun (Praj-nacakra) in 861, and by Shih-hu (Danapala) around 990. These Chinese translations of the longer version are all quite similar, except for the second, retranslation by Fa-yueh, which includes just enough window dressing to make one wonder if his Tantric hosts in Ch'ang-an did not at some point encourage him to "add feet to his snake." Aside from this singular anomaly, the Chinese translations of the longer version agree quite closely with the Sanskrit edition edited by Conze, which is the edition I have used for the following translation.

The only significant difference between the longer and shorter versions of the text, and this applies to the Chinese as well as the Sanskrit, is that the longer version includes an intro-duction and conclusion, thus serving to elevate this from a dha-rani to the standard sutra format. The rest of the text, as a quick comparison with the shorter version at the front of this book will show, was identical.

Thus have I heard: Once when the Bhagavan was dwelling on Rajgir's Vulture Mountain together with a great assembly of bhikshus and a great assembly of bodhisattvas, he entered the samadhi known as Manifestation of the Deep. At that moment, the fearless Avalokiteshvara Bodhisattva was practicing the deep practice of Prajnaparamita, and looking upon the Five Skandhas saw that they were empty of self-existence. By the power of the Buddha, the venerable Shariputra then asked the fearless Avalokiteshvara Bodhisattva, "If any noble son or daughter were to practice the deep practice of Prajnaparamita, how should they be instructed?"

Avalokiteshvara Bodhisattva answered, "Shariputra, if any noble son or daughter were to practice the deep practice of Prajnaparamita, they should thus be instructed: 'empty of self-existence are the Five Skandhas.'

"Here, Shariputra, form is emptiness, emptiness is form; emptiness is not separate from form, form is not separate from emptiness; whatever is form is emptiness, whatever is emptiness is form. The same holds for sensation and perception, memory and consciousness. Here, Shariputra, all dharmas are defined by emptiness, not birth or destruction, purity or defilement, completeness or deficiency.

"Therefore, Shariputra, in emptiness there is no form, no sensation, no perception, no memory and no consciousness; no eye, no ear, no nose, no tongue, no body and no mind; no shape, no sound, no smell, no taste, no feeling and no thought; no element of perception, from eye to conceptual consciousness; no causal link, from ignorance to old age and death, and no end of causal link, from ignorance to old age and death; no suffering, no source, no relief, no path; no knowledge, no attainment and no non-attainment.

"Therefore, Shariputra, without attainment, bodhisattvas take refuge in Prajnaparamita and live without walls of the mind. Without walls of the mind and thus without fears, they see through delusions and finally nirvana. All buddhas past, present, and future also take refuge in Prajnaparamita and realize unexcelled, perfect enlightenment.

"You should therefore know the great mantra of Prajnaparamita, the mantra of great magic, the unexcelled mantra, the mantra equal to the unequalled, which heals all suffering and is true, not false, the mantra in Prajnaparamita spoken thus:

"'*Gate gate, para-gate, para-san-gate, bodhi svaha.*'

"Thus, Shariputra, should fearless bodhisattvas be instructed to practice the deep practice of Prajnaparamita."

At that moment, the Bhagavan rose from samadhi and praised Avalokiteshvara Bodhisattva, "Well done, noble son, well done. So it is, noble son, so should the deep practice of Prajnaparamita be practiced. As you have declared, so is it confirmed by all arhats and tathagatas."

When the Bhagavan had finished speaking, the venerable Shariputra, the fearless Avalokiteshvara Bodhisattva, and all those present in the worlds of gods, humans, asuras, and gandharvas praised what the Bhagavan had proclaimed.

Thus concludes the *Heart of Prajnaparamita*.